Guitar/Vocal

Authentic
GUITAR-TAB
Edition ™
Complete Solos

CLASSIC
LED ZEPPELIN
HOUSES OF THE HOLY

Transcribed and Arranged by Hemme Luttjeboer

© 1993 WARNER BROS. PUBLICATIONS INC.
All Rights Reserved
Printed in Canada

Contents

Key To Notation Symbols

4

Foreword

"HOUSES OF THE HOLY" represents a non-conventional Led Zeppelin release in that it is their first with a title and their first to include complete lyrics [Led Zeppelin IV only included the lyrics to "Stairway To Heaven"]. It was recorded between January and August 1972, at a time when the band was at their prime. "Stairway To Heaven", fast becoming a rock anthem, afforded Led Zeppelin the time to leisurely develop a follow-up recording.

An inspirational trip to Bombay, India to record with Indian musicians preceded the laying of initial tracks at Stargroves, a country house owned by Mick Jagger. Using the Rolling Stones Mobile at first, "Houses Of The Holy" was eventually finished at Olympic Studios in London and Electric Lady in New York. The actual rollicking title track, deleted from this album named for it, however, later appeared on "Physical Graffiti."

Hemme B. Luttjeboer

Performance Notes

The Song Remains The Same

After using working titles such as "The Overture" and "The Campaign", the opening number turned into "The Song Remains The Same" after Robert Plant added his lyrics; Led Zeppelin's tribute to world music. Jimmy Page had been working on an intricate piece of music with multiple guitars, shifting tempos and changing atmospheres. The intro hints at what we are to expect.

There are basically five distinct sections within this tune, each leap-frogging throughout. Because of it's structure, rehearsal letters have been designated to each one for easy reference.

Jimmy tastefully doubles a 12-string figure throughout the intensely rhythmic intro, accenting the 4th beat voicings. An eight-measure A section deftly utilizes space and resolves to letter B. After establishing a repeated four measure phrase in D major, he shifts momentarily into a ii-v in C major for four bars. Here he rhythmically pedals F natural with his pick as his fingers play a melody. A folkish influence inspired by British guitarist, Bert Jansch.

Section D reinstates the key center of the tune and sets up Jimmy's first solo at E. Sustaining this section using arpeggios, Page lets loose with ideas based on D major pentatonic. The tempo climaxes and breathes at rehearsal letter F with a half-time feel as Plant begins his first verse. A somewhat country feel in G major is augmented by Jimmy's double-tracked arpeggios and background guitar with clean tone bends. Verse 1 ends with

a retreat into double-time, segueing into Page's second solo at H.

At J, Jimmy entertains us with his stylistic A minor pentatonic ideas for eight measures and Robert Plant echoes the theme of the tune at K for another eight. This whole section climaxes with a heavily-doubled D6 arpeggiation and takes us to the sixteen-bar L section. Again, with a country tinge, Page seasons the arpeggiated harmony with G major pentatonic bends, shifting momentarily to C major pentatonic and E Aeolian [key of G major.]

His third solo takes off with A major pentatonic [F minor] ideas including a brief hint at A major Ionian. Page favors A major pentatonic, but soon leans toward A minor pentatonic as the progression nears rehearsal letter N. Here he decorates the D major tonal center with a flourish of D major pentatonic tones.

At letter O, Page plays a four measure A pentatonic line before lashing into A5. Using his stylistic Zeppelin sound, he repeats a phrase based on A major pentatonic. Plant returns at the D.S., revealing the band's influence from India as he vocalizes into the Coda, thus ending a lengthy opener.

The Rain Song

Jimmy Page's experimentation with non-standard tunings yielded this hauntingly sensitive, quasi-blues ballad. Coupled with Robert Plant's infatuation with "Celtic mysticism" it is a highly structured composition that makes use of open-string chordal movements involving tension and release phrases. It displays Page's leanings for diverse styles such as the blues, folk, lounge-jazz, etc. Painstakingly constructed, it is backdropped by the mellotron of John Paul Jones, by now a stage prop as well.

Both guitars, acoustic and six-string Danelectro, are tuned in a Gsus4 tuning; a result of Jimmy's noodling for different textures. You should be able to play through the piece by focussing on the tablature. The opening strains are sustained by the use of open strings as your left hand moves toward G7 and resolves unexpectedly to E♭/G. This resolution could be viewed as a brief iv minor plagal cadence [Cm7 with no root] before proceeding to G6. The A♭9 to G9 slide augments the "blue" atmosphere. Notice the standard, all-to-familiar chord shapes that yield different sounds in this tuning?

Page's descending single line on electric at the close of the first verse is doubled slightly out of sync. The soft subtle tones give way to a harsher, climactic sixteen-measure bridge as Plant reaffirms his feelings. It is short-lived, however, as a return to the initial ambience takes us through the fourth verse. Page closes the tune with the last twelve bars, doubling the acoustic arpeggios on electric. The slightly dissonant G7+11 yields to the more consonant pedalled C major melodies as Page descends and elects to resolve to Gsus2. Bonham's role is subtle yet effective using brushes throughout the tune, as is the stirring sound projected by John Paul Jones on mellotron.

OVER THE HILLS AND FAR AWAY

The acoustic guitar is once again at the forefront of a Zeppelin masterpiece. Showcasing Jimmy Page's prowess, the influence and fondness for the music and styles of British guitarist Bert Jansch are apparent. The folkish ambience in the intro and first verse subside to an electric attack in the second and subsequent sections. Combining diverse styles into one composition is an already established characteristic of Led Zeppelin music.

The definable acoustic signature based in G major, is doubled in the tenth measure by a twelve-string guitar, tastefully filling out the motif. The songsmith's panache is clearly shown through the first verse accompanying Robert Plant's vocals. Jimmy builds the acoustic tracks by climbing up the neck with triadic voicings. A slightly harder edge, brought to life by the entry of bass, drums and electric guitar, introduces the second, third and fourth verses in D major.

Jimmy's overdubbed guitar solo is based in F# minor as he gives himself harmonic support with a repetitive double-stopped measure. The first six measures concede to his lines an octave higher based on F# minor pentatonic, complete with stylistic "Pagean" phrasing. The ascending, harmonized F#7 arpeggio in 3/4 time is cleverly supported by Bonham's 4/4 drum beat. Their interest in odd time signatures and different time/feel superimpositions are now an integral part of the Zeppelin style.

A novel approach for a deceptive ending has John Paul Jones improvising the intro theme on keyboards. The last four measures, written here for guitar, descend to a G major resolution with pedal steel sounds, also arranged for six-string guitar. Yet another display of Page's affinity for that "country" flavor.

THE CRUNGE

John [Bonzo] Bonham's influence and contribution lead to the creation of this tune. Born from a rehearsal "jam" while at Stargroves, the 9/8 drum pattern became the focal point for the James Brown parody. With Page mimicking the funkmeister's guitarist, Jimmy Nolen, Plant's vocal ad lib, and Jones' bass and synth lines, what we hear is Led Zeppelin's tongue-in-cheek emulation of a Stax/Motown funk band complete with a horn section.

The shifting time signatures can be tough at first, jumping from 9/8, 4/4, 5/8, to 2/4. Follow Plant's vocals to assist you and/or subdivide 9/8 to 1-2, 1-2, 1-2, 1-2-3. Jones' bass line joins Bonham's drum figure in the intro with further accompaniment from Page's bright sounding three-note "Nolen" chords.

The intensity of the the 9/8 measures resolves to straight 4/4 time with a D9 chord change, succumbing, however, to 5/8 and 2/4. These two bars can be counted as 9/8, but clearly accent the "punches" as written accordingly.

Jones' contribution, aside from his ongoing bass support, is elaborated on

synth. Written here for guitar(s), they are simple and effective Motown horn lines, once again revealing the band's American music influence. The humor is evident in the last nine measures as Plant impatiently awaits the "bridge" that never appears.

DANCING DAYS

Reflecting Led Zeppelin's feelings for the time spent at Stargroves in rehearsal, "Dancing Days" is a culmination and product of inspiration from the experience in India. The opening measure, played by electric guitar with a slide, denotes a Lydian tonality. Page was influenced by the sound of the shenai, an Indian double-reed wind instrument. Guitar 1 is accompanied by an electric guitar in a G tuning. As a result of this tuning, Page manages to sound the spirited, upper partial full-range voicings that he plays at the first verse. Watch the tablature carefully. A keyboard part, played by Jones, doubles this part in the third verse and continues with the same figure throughout the fourth verse as Jimmy comps with simple root-five and root-six dyads in support.

An eight-measure recapitulation of the intro theme is followed by Jimmy's guitar solo. Guitar 1 is actually performed by two separate guitars with slide, while Guitar 2 continues with its harmonic support. The slide figure can be played by one guitar but has been arranged here as recorded. Jimmy simply works his way up the neck in thirds and asserts the intro's hypnotic motif an octave higher until the fine.

D'YER MAK'ER

Probably the most commercial contribution by Led Zeppelin ever, "D'Yer Mak'er" started as a reggae but ended up as a '50s parody. The title actually comes from an old joke and play on "Jamaica". [The second tongue-in-cheek ditty on the album].

At this time in 1972, Jamaican reggae was fast becoming the sensation in England. Bob Marley and The Wailers had relocated there as well. Plant adored the '50s music, á la Ricky Nelson, so the next logical step was to write a tune in that style. To play along with the recording, tune your guitar down about 1/4 tone to match the correct pitch.

Jimmy plays a somewhat sloppy and slightly distorted, palm-muted I-vi-IV-V progression that he injects with arpeggios and 6th slides. Jones' piano accents the off-beats. Plant's mindless lyrics reflect the bygone era of the '50s with his lamentations of love. Bonham kicks the piece off and gives his heavy-handed support in 4/4 time.

Jimmy never sticks to a definite pattern as he repeats the progression. At the chorus, a vi-V-IV-V chord sequence, a more Zeppelin-type sound is introduced via Jimmy's choice of guitar voicings. Yet, they give way to more arpeggios as we return to another verse.

After the second chorus, Page entertains us with a brief eight-bar solo. He remains very true diatonically to the key of C major, shifting in and around A Aeolian and A minor pentatonic; a well-crafted musical statement that climaxes with a high E note. The progression is repeated until it fades out to conclude the piece.

Simple, trite and unlike any of the other compositions on "Houses Of The Holy" it does keep in line with the general flow of the album; the absence of any real "hard rock."

NO QUARTER

During the recording of the album, John Paul Jones exploited his musical sensitivity and palette by sprinkling various tonal colors on each tune. He contributed this piece, the second longest next to "The Rain Song", a quiet and solemn effort.

Jones introduces the tune, in C#m with electric piano/mellotron and states the main theme twice before Page and Bonham add their support. The keyboard figure has been arranged here for one guitar, hopefully capturing the essence of the melody. The repeated chorus section is reinforced by Page's thick and heavy fuzz-toned guitar line.

A return to the main theme by Jones leads us to the first verse where an inspired Robert Plant sings about a Viking death squad, riding the wings of Thor to some desperate Satanic destiny. Jones' song proved to be an excellent vehicle for the Celtic images that influenced Plant. Jimmy's guitar role up to this point is sparse except for the chorus and the A(addD#) and D(addG#) chords.

A piano improvisation by Jones over a C#m7 comp for sixteen measures makes way for Bonham's setup of Jimmy's guitar solo. With everything laid back and spacious, Page lashes out with some hip, clean-toned C# minor pentatonic and G# minor pentatonic ideas. A second guitar with a thick fuzz-tone compliments his first clean-toned statement by mimicking his final thought. Page responds with sextuplets based on G# minor pentatonic and the second guitar reacts with a C# Aeolian line. Elements of C# minor pentatonic, C# blues and G# minor pentatonic form Jimmy's subsequent barrage of single notes as he winds up his clean-tone solo with octaves. The second guitar resumes the solo with typical Page phrasing, focussing on a C# Dorian sound as well as C# minor pentatonic tones.

Robert Plant vocalizes as Jones restates the main keyboard theme through the last verse, as Page and Bonham man their posts for the final twenty-four-measure chorus before fading out.

THE OCEAN

Pre-recording banter by John Bonham: "We've four already, but now we're steady, and then they went, 'one, two, three, four...'" typifies the relaxed atmosphere during the Stargrove sessions. This tune is Robert Plant's image of the hot and sweaty crowds that, from the stage, appeared to sway back and forth like "ocean" waves.

Alternating between 4/4 and 7/8 time in the intro, Page deftly syncopates the "hook" with sixteenth notes. If you run into trouble counting 7/8, subdivide the beats 1-2, 1-2, 1-2-3 and/or just listen enough times to "feel" the groove. Based on A major, Page continues with sixteenth note triads in the verse section but uses a measure of 7/8 to launch him back into the intro figure. After the second verse, he solos over the alternating 4/4 to 7/8 hook.

Centered around A minor pentatonic, he solos with his classic Les Paul tone. An eight-measure verse section follows as Page layers the ensuing harmony with guitars. The resulting sound elaborates the previous triadic accompaniment into four-part harmony. Plant tones things down with an eight-bar a cappella.

In the final chorus, Jimmy plays the guitar figure with a bit more intensity, using a heavier palm mute, anticipating the upcoming section.

At a faster tempo, this outro has a 12/8 [triplet] feel and takes us through the final thirty-six measures of the tune. Divided into three twelve-bar lengths, each chorus has a "tag." For accompaniment, Page uses triplets shifting between a D triad and an E triad on one guitar while he solos primarily in A major on another. The four-measure "tag" is based on an A major scale and is subsequently harmonized in 6ths and 5ths.

Robert Plant affirms the "good" feeling experienced at the end of the last twelve bars. Rock 'N Roll heard at its best, by the best... Led Zeppelin.

HBL

The Song Remains The Same

Words and Music by
JIMMY PAGE and ROBERT PLANT

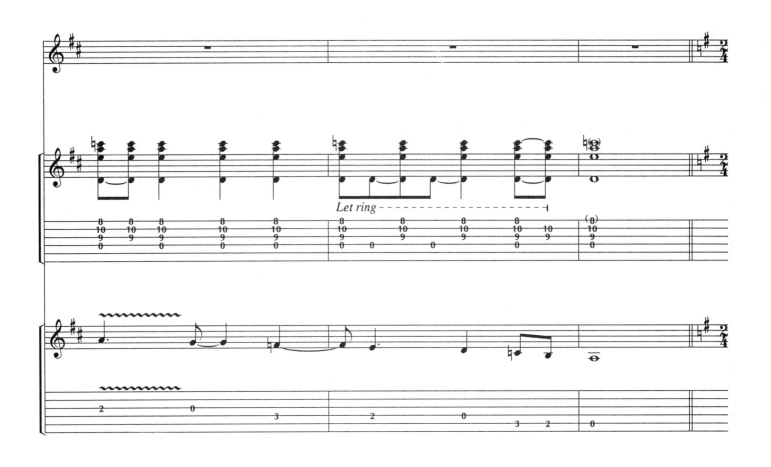

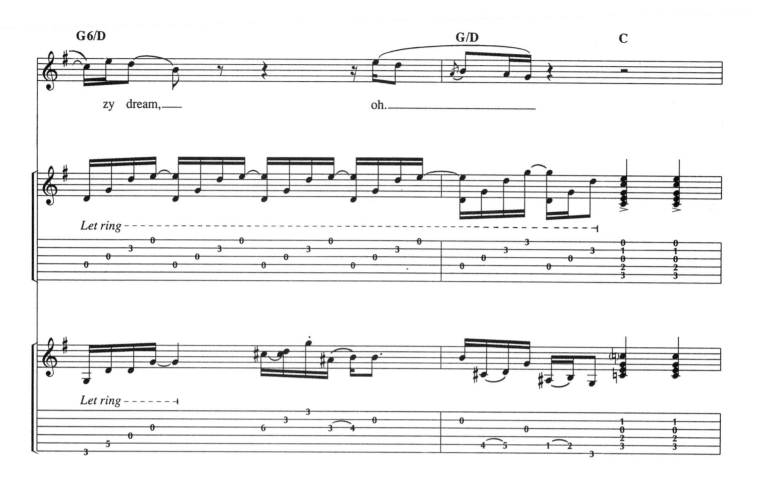

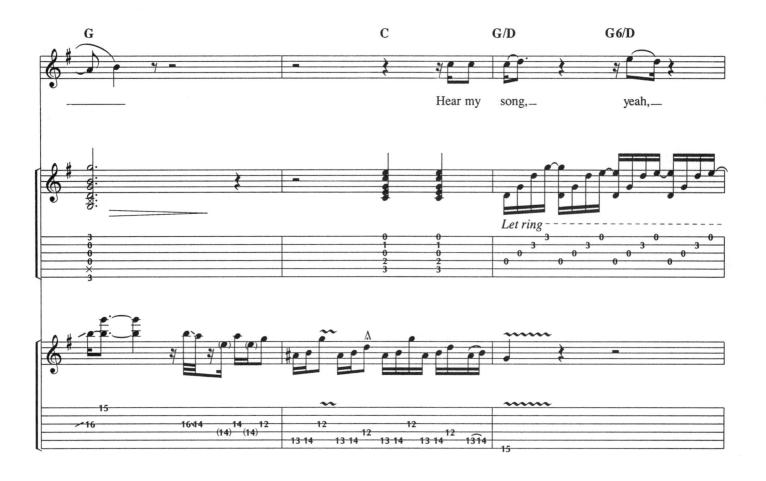

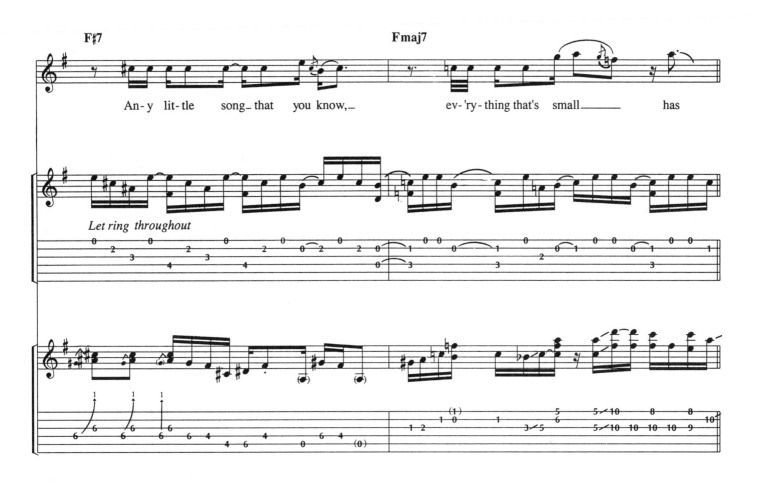

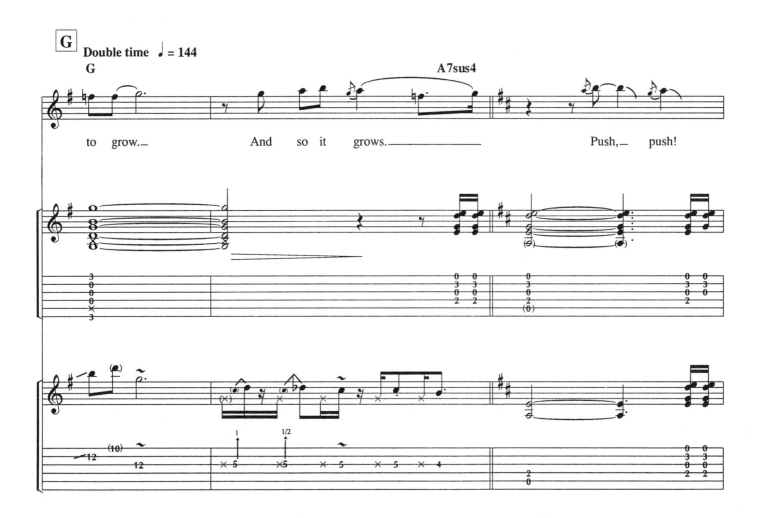

All - right.

A7sus4

A7sus4(addF♯)

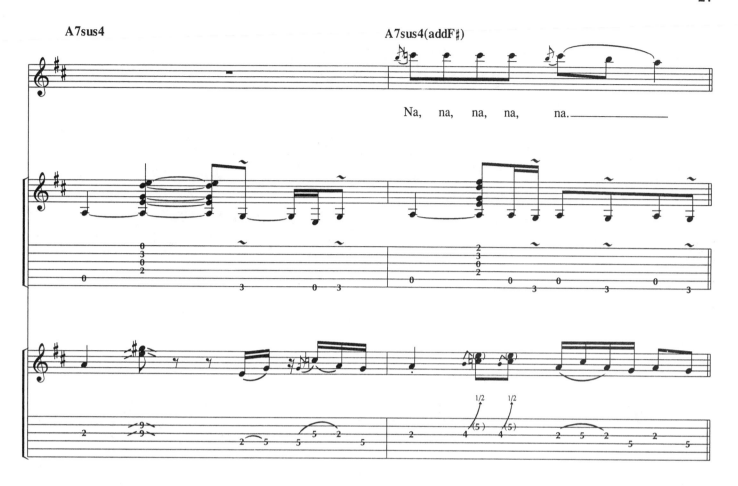

Na, na, na, na, na._____

With Fill 1 on D.S. only.

K 𝄋

D   G/D   D   Em   D

Cal - i - for - nia sun - light,   sweet__ Cal - cut - ta__ rain.__
Sing__ out har - e, har - e,   oo,__ an' dance__ the Hoot-chie Koo..

Guitars 1 & 2

Let ring throughout

Fill 1

Guitar 3

f

Hon-o-lu - lu___ star - bright,___
Cit- y lights___ are, oh, so bright,___

Guitar 1

Guitar 3

the song___ re - mains___ the same.___
as we go___ slid - ing, slid - ing, a slid - ing, slid-ing, a, slid-

Let ring - - - - - - - -

Fade in

ing, a,— slid - ing, a,— slid - ing, slid-ing, a, slide. Oo,

oh,————— ho, ho.

To Coda ⊕

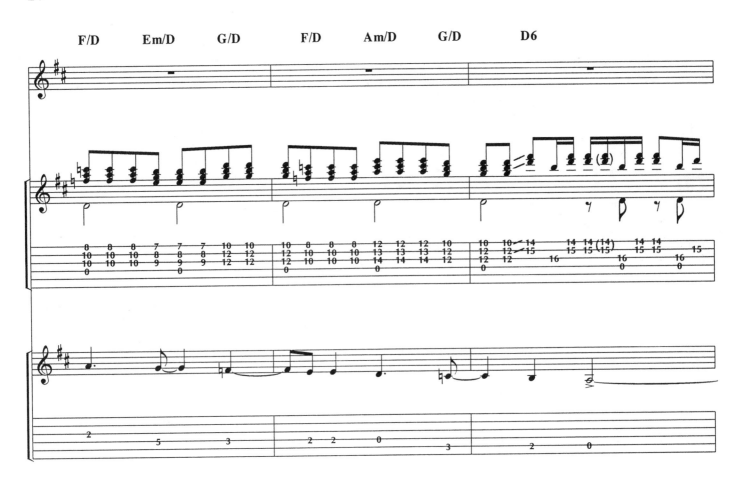

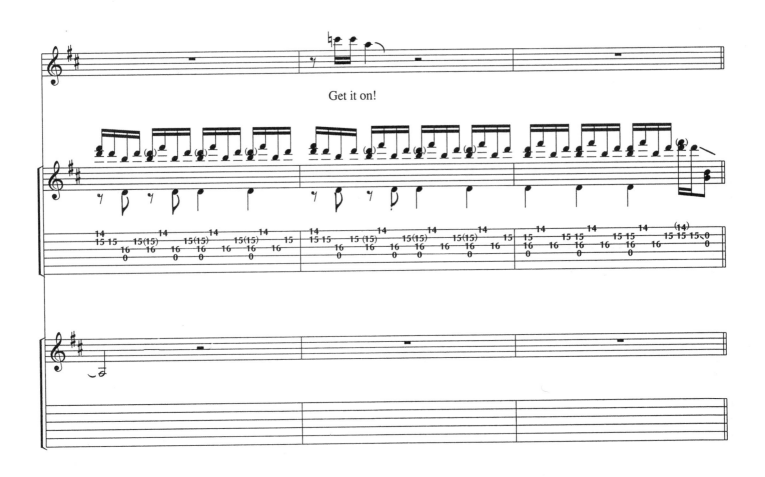

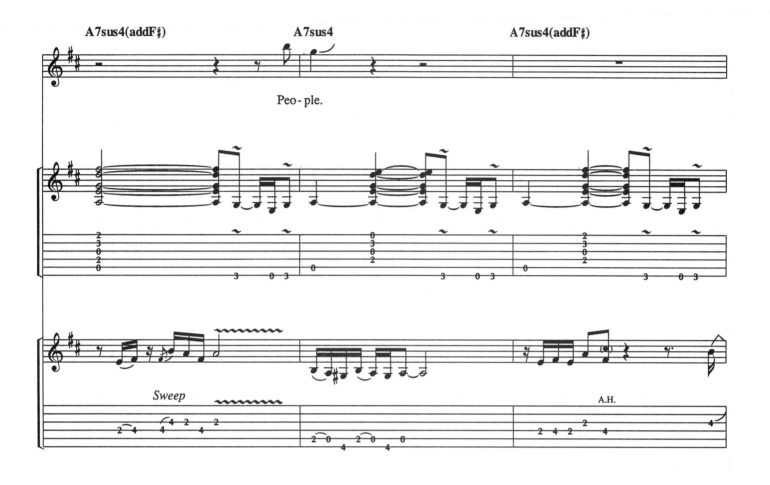

Peo- ple.

Sweep

A.H.

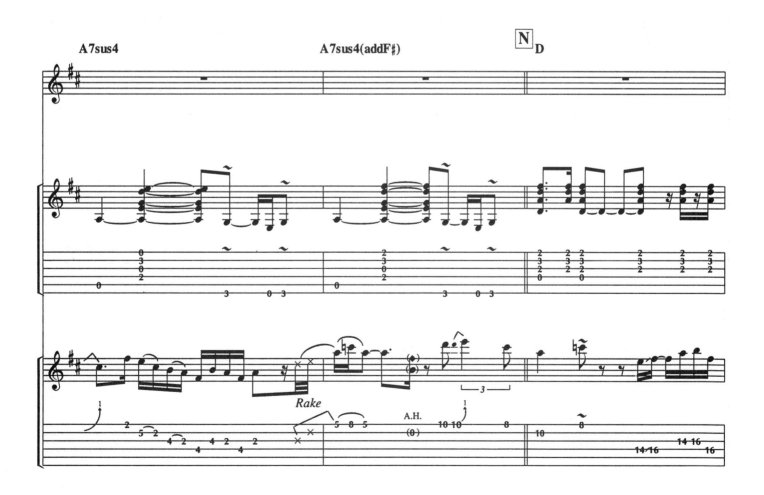

Rake

A.H.

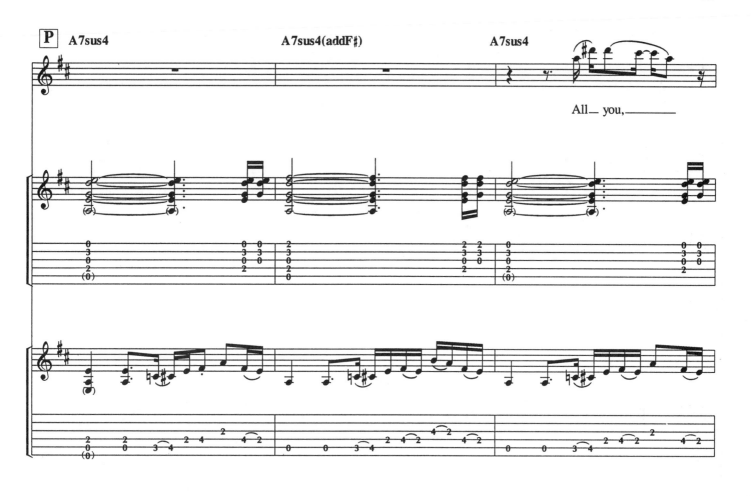

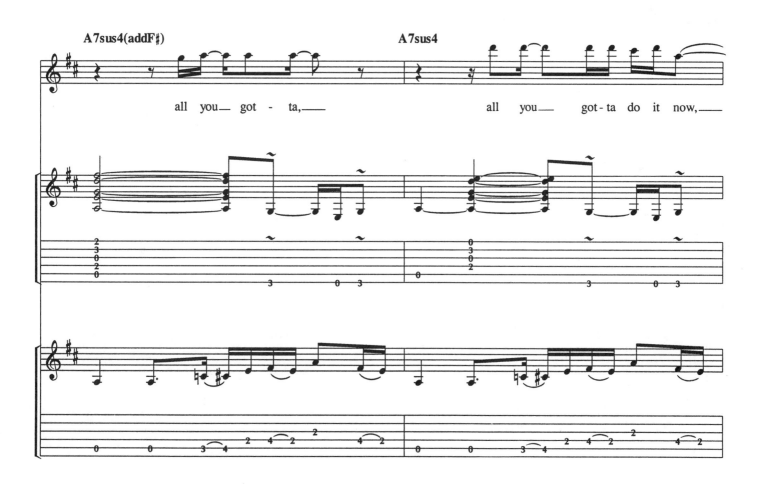

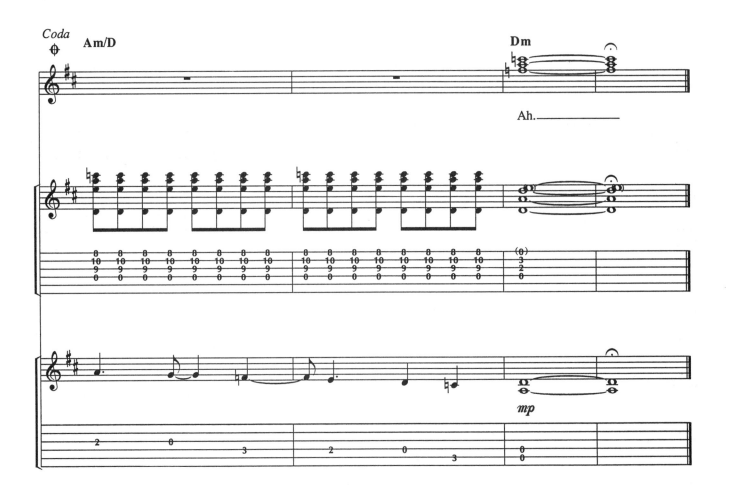

The Rain Song

Words and Music by
JIMMY PAGE and ROBERT PLANT

Moderate ballad ♩ = 74
Intro:

* *Acoustic and Electric Guitars in Gsus4 tuning.* ⑥ = D, ⑤ = G, ④ = C, ③ = G, ② = C, ① = D

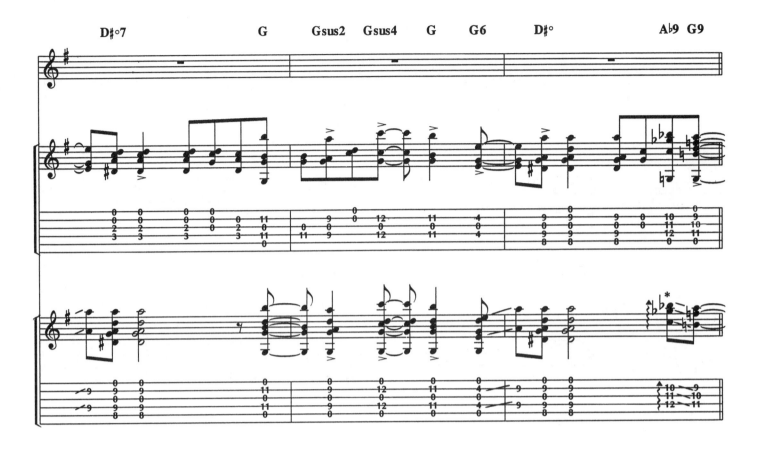

Verse 1:

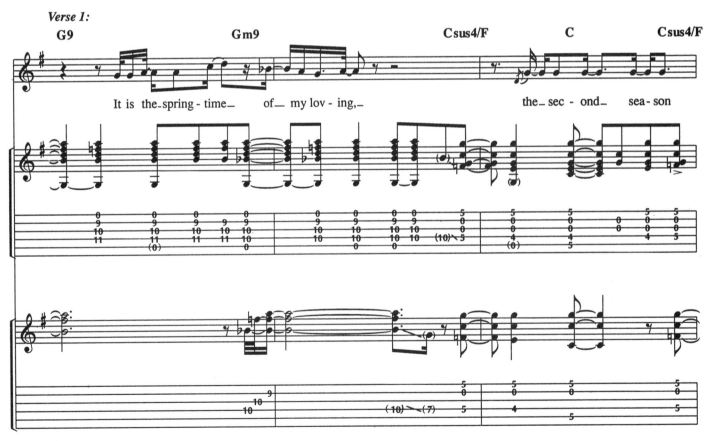

Overdub

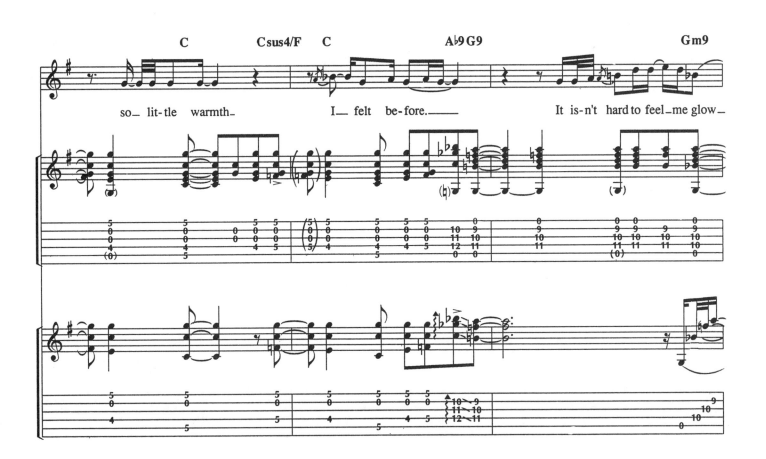

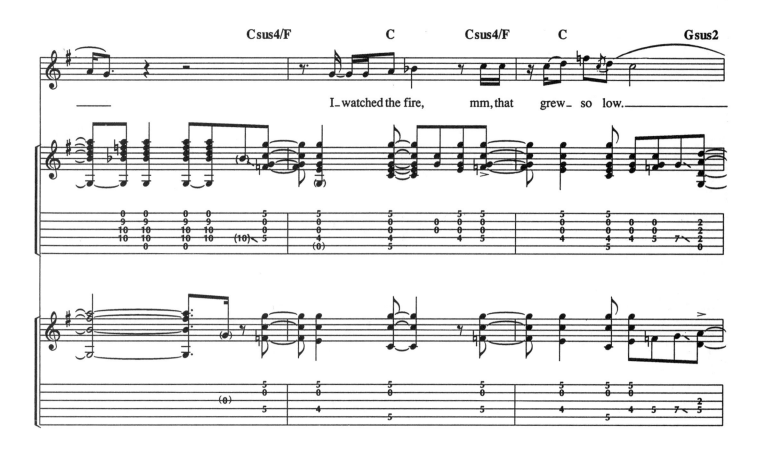

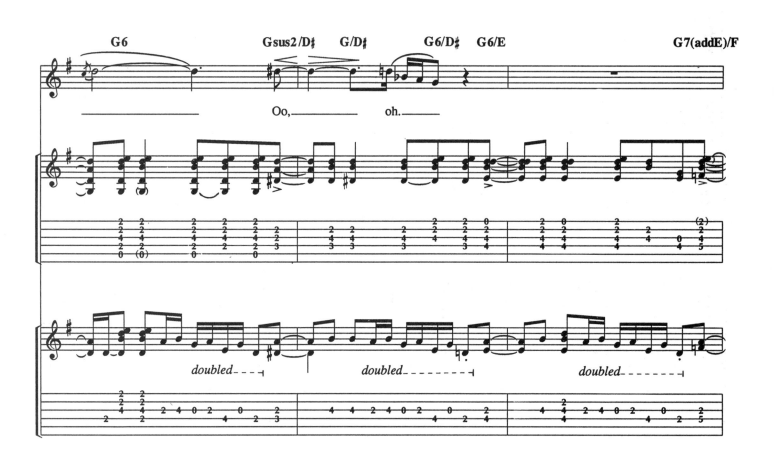

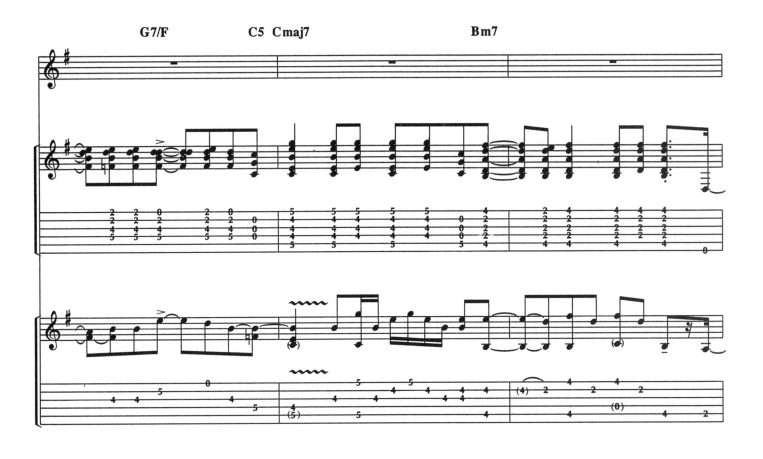

* Overdub

* Overdub

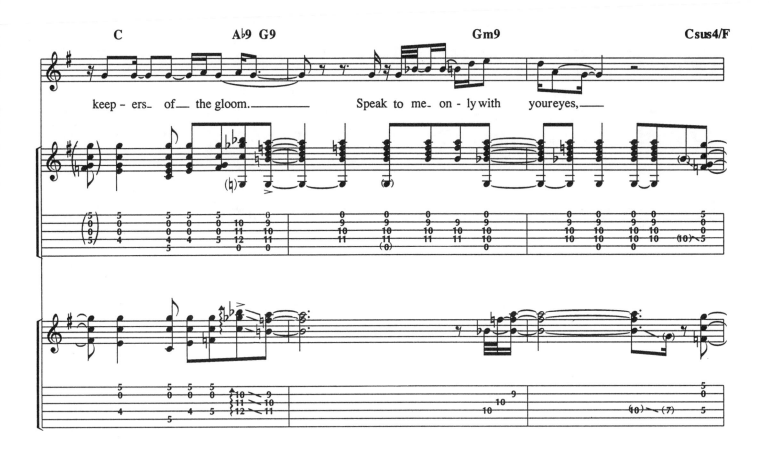

keep - ers_ of_ the gloom._____ Speak to me_ on - ly with youreyes,___

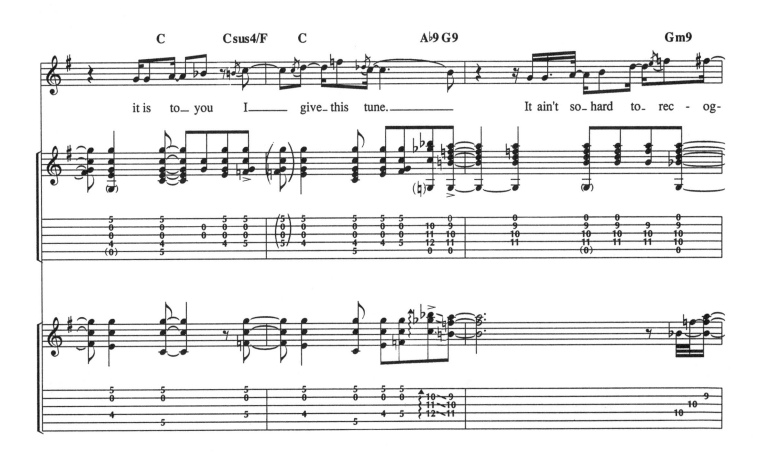

it is to_ you I_____ give_ this tune._____ It ain't so_ hard to_ rec - og-

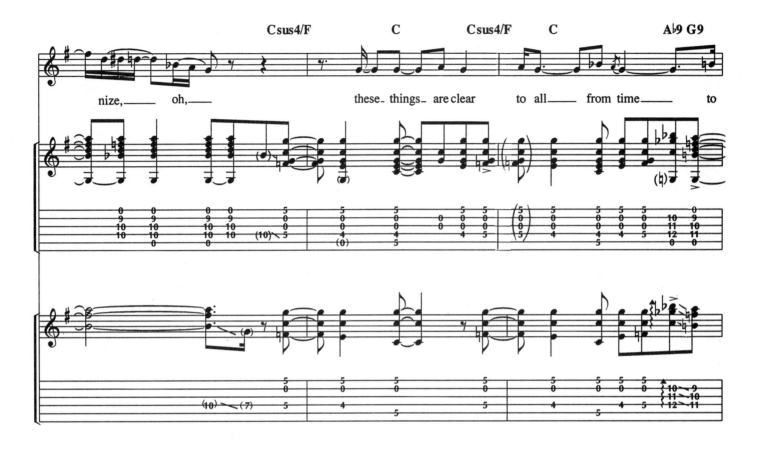

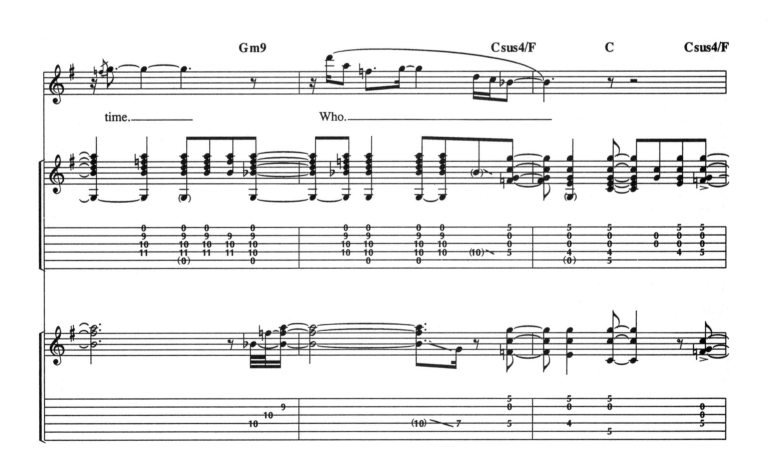

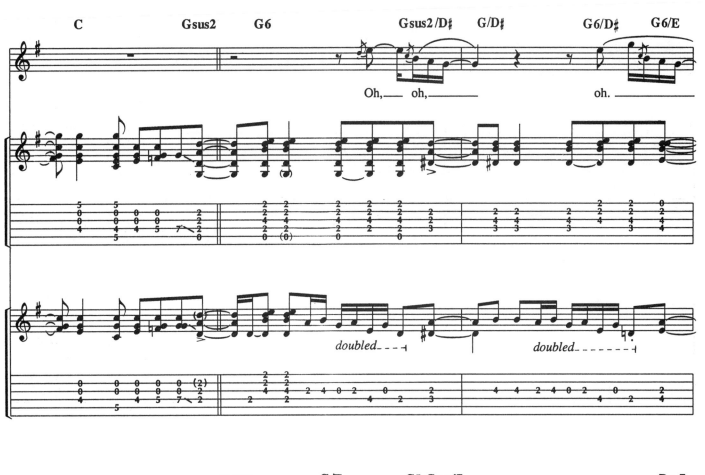

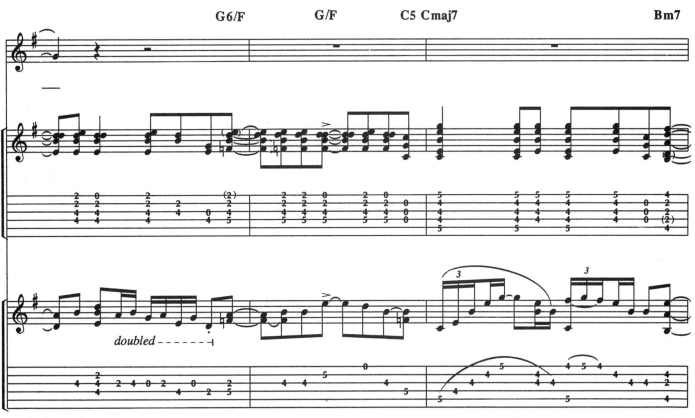

Am11/D

poco ritard.

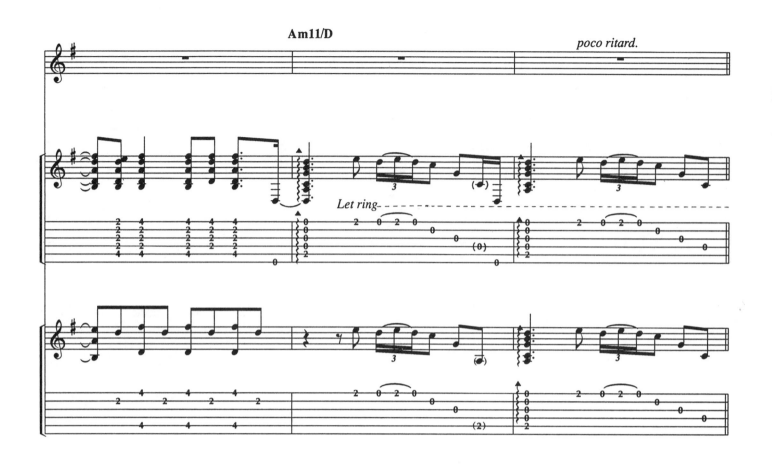

Bridge:
a tempo

G5　　　　　**F5**　　　　　**C5**　　　　　**G5**

Ah!　　　Talk,　talk,＿＿＿ talk,＿＿ talk.＿＿

mf

f Dirty tone

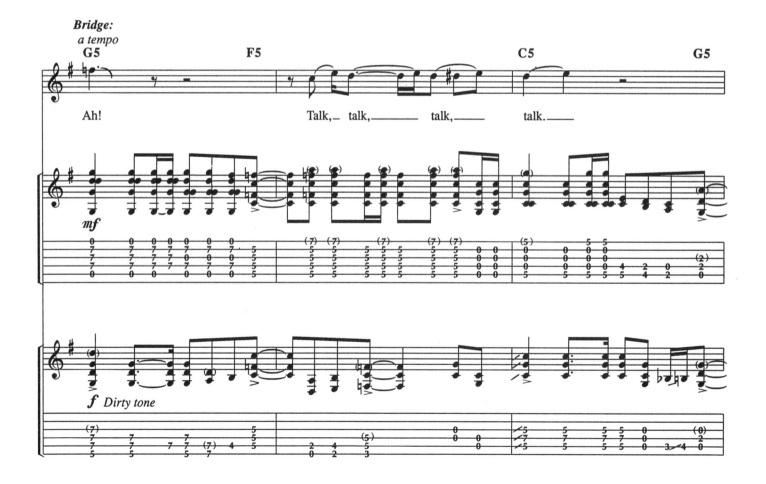

Verse 3:

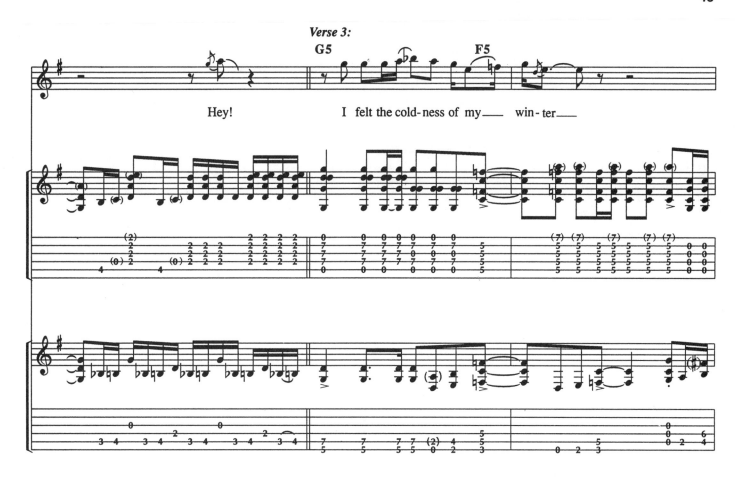

Hey!   I felt the cold-ness of my___ win-ter___

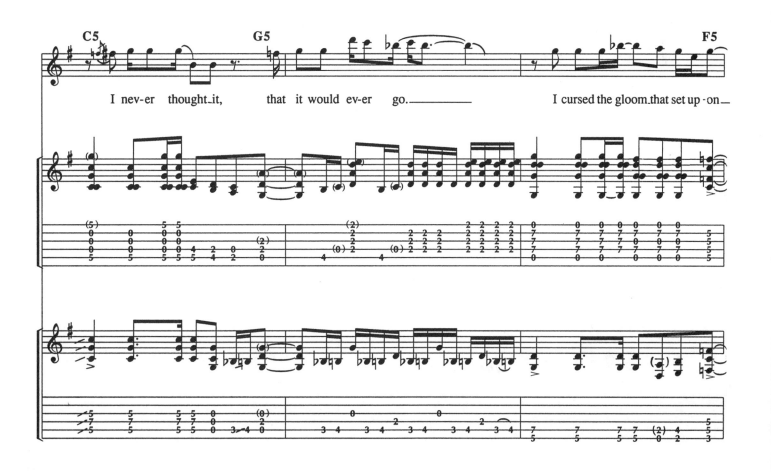

I nev-er thought it,   that it would ev-er go.___   I cursed the gloom that set up-on___

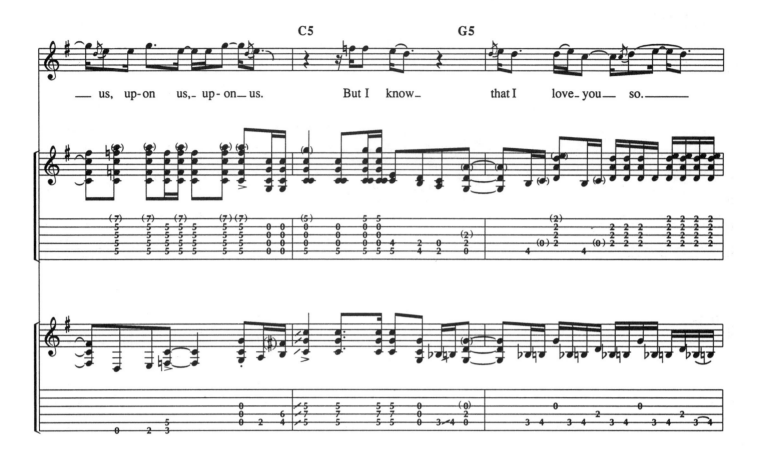

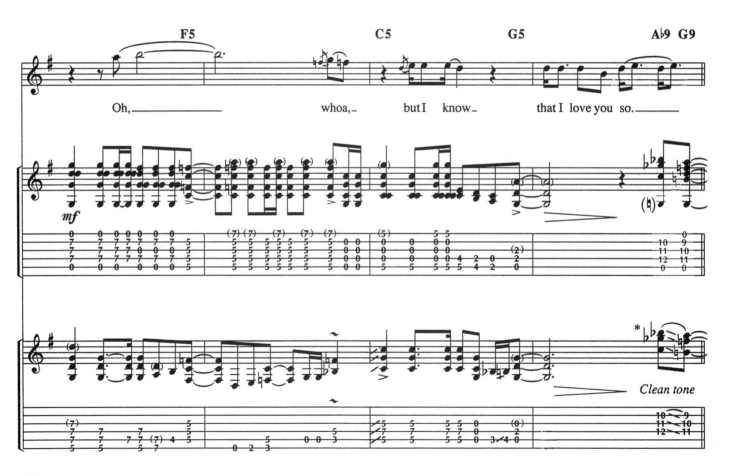

*Overdub

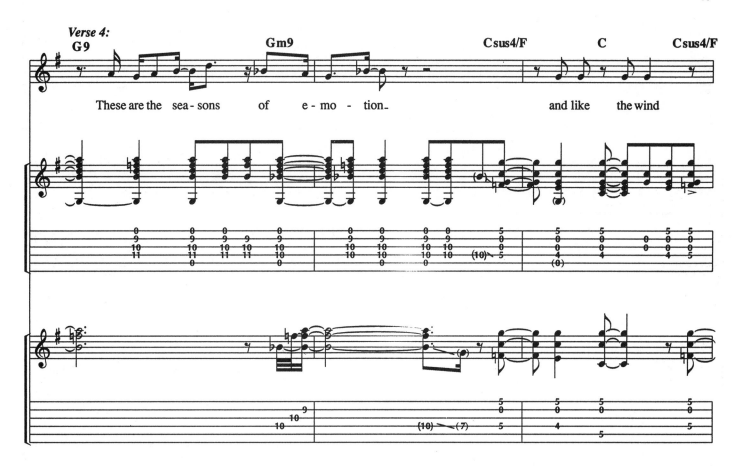

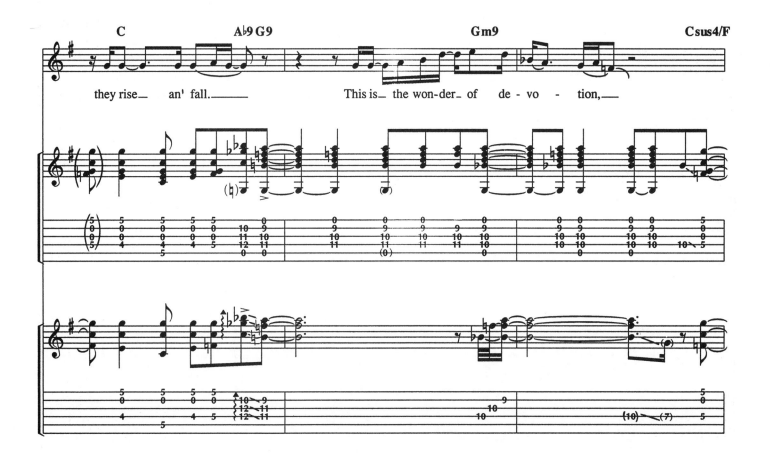

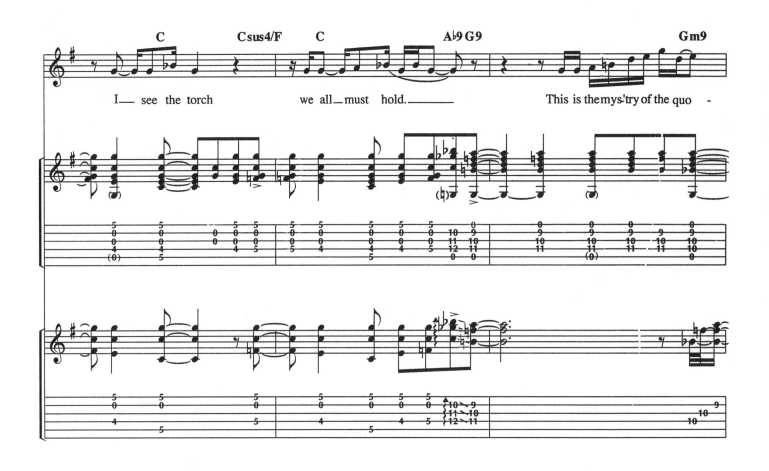

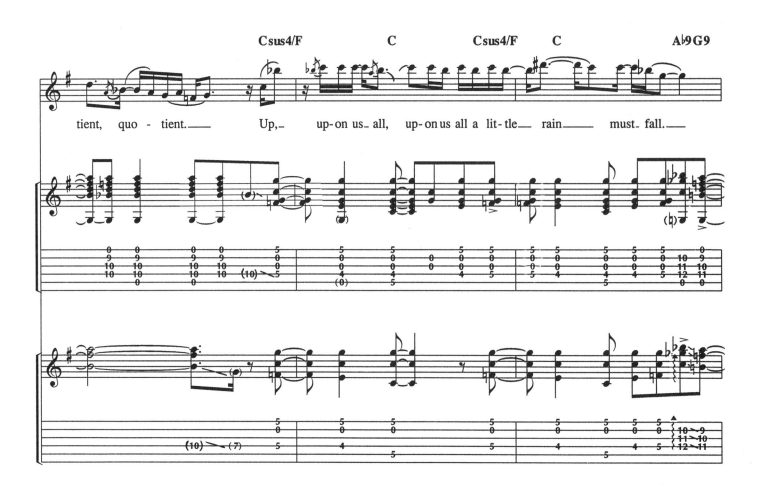

A, just a lit-tle rain._____ Ho,_____ yeah! Oh!

Oo,___ yeah_yeah_yeah!___

doubled---| doubled----------|

*Doubled on acoustic.

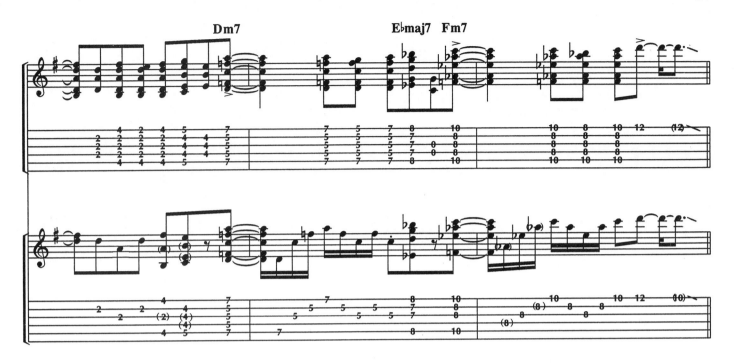

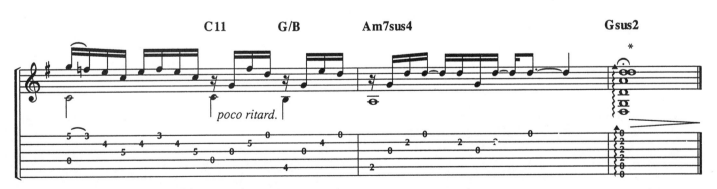

*Guitar 2 fades out with echo delay repeats.

Over The Hills And Far Away

Words and Music by
JIMMY PAGE and ROBERT PLANT

Moderately fast Rock (♩ = 98)
Intro:
Guitar 1* (Acoustic 6 string)

* 12 string guitar doubles on repeat and Verse 1.

Fill 1
Guitar 2 (12 string)

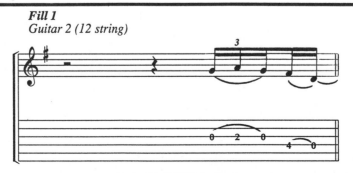

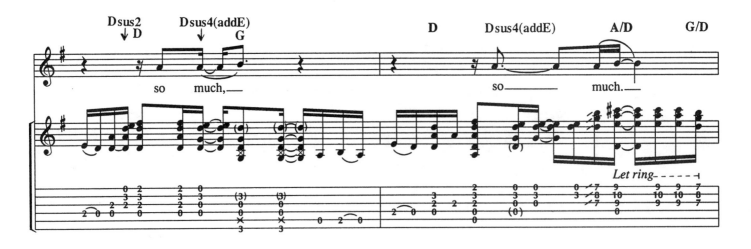

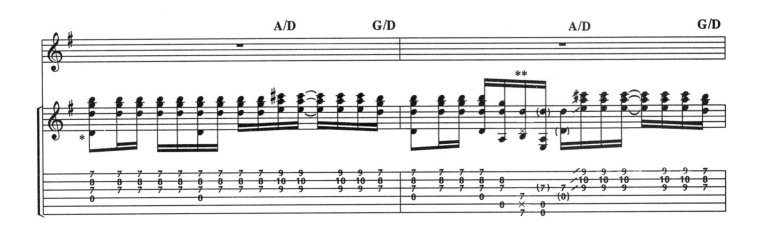

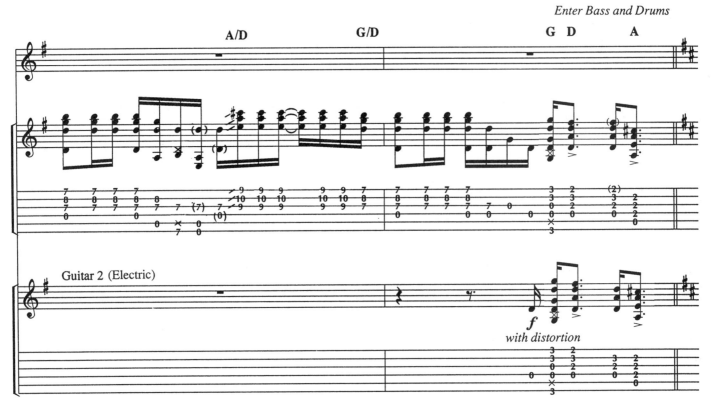

*Let 4th string ring out.
** With thumb.

Verses 2, 3:

12 String Guitar tacet

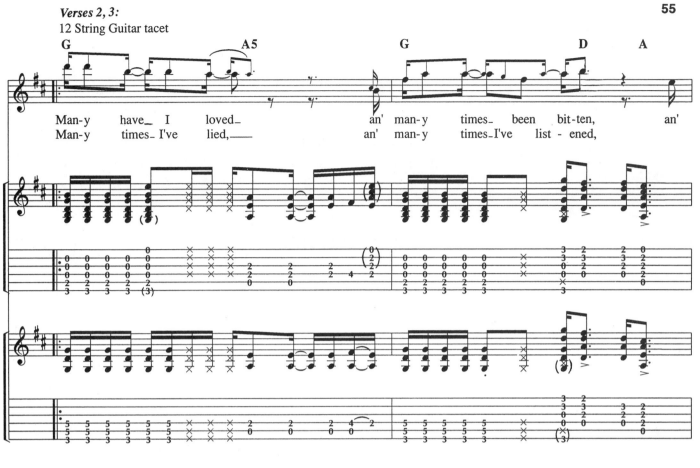

Man-y have I loved an' man-y times been bit-ten, an'
Man-y times I've lied, an' man-y times I've list-ened,

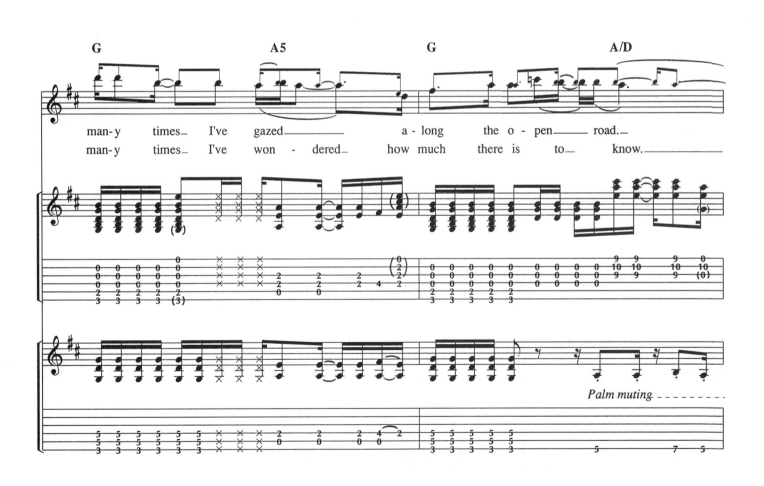

man-y times I've gazed a-long the o-pen road.
man-y times I've won-dered how much there is to know.

Palm muting - - - - - - - - -

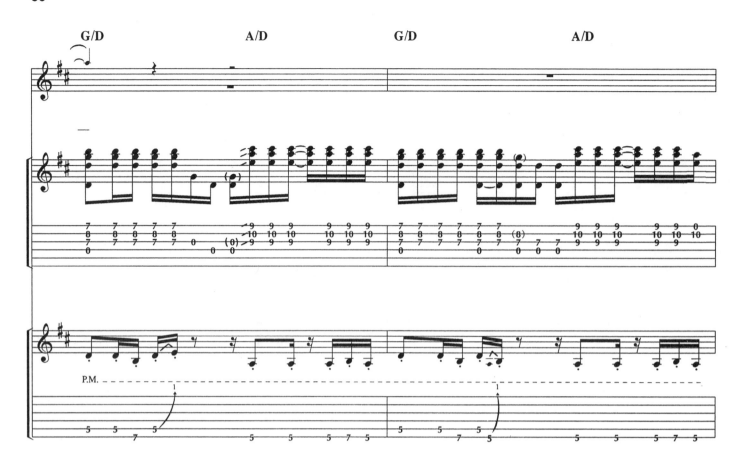

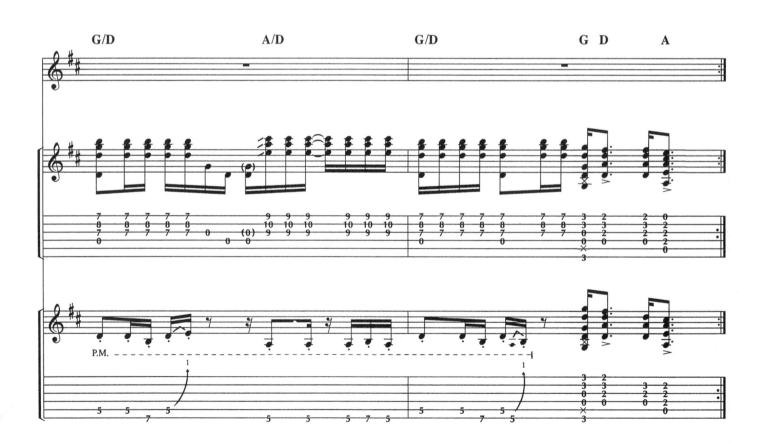

Verse 4:

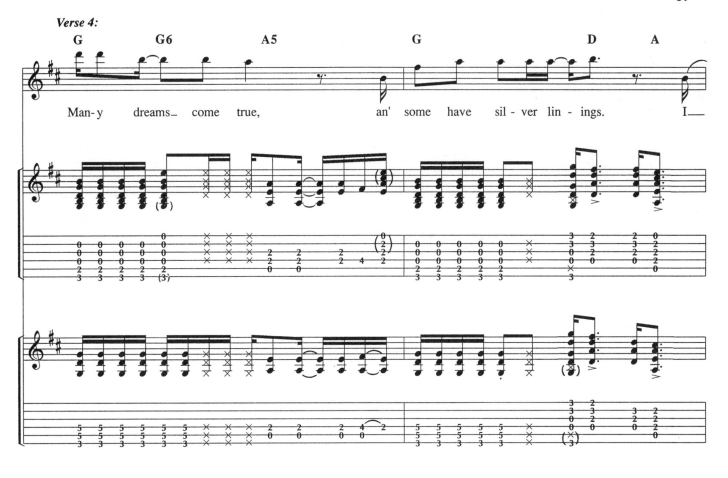

Man-y dreams— come true, an' some have sil - ver lin - ings. I—

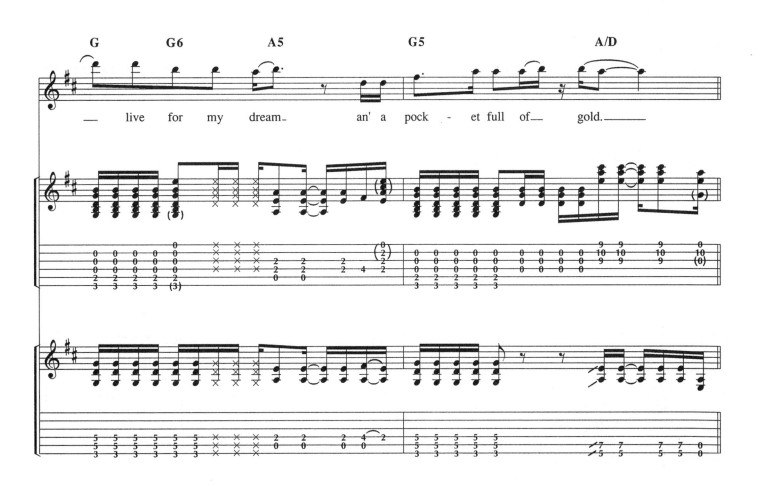

— live for my dream— an' a pock - et full of— gold.———

* *Guitar 3-downstem notes*
  Guitar 4-upstem notes

(F♯)

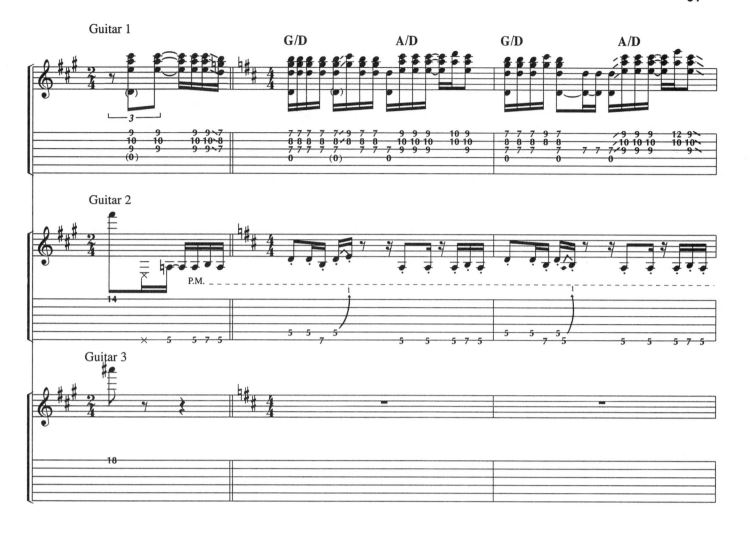

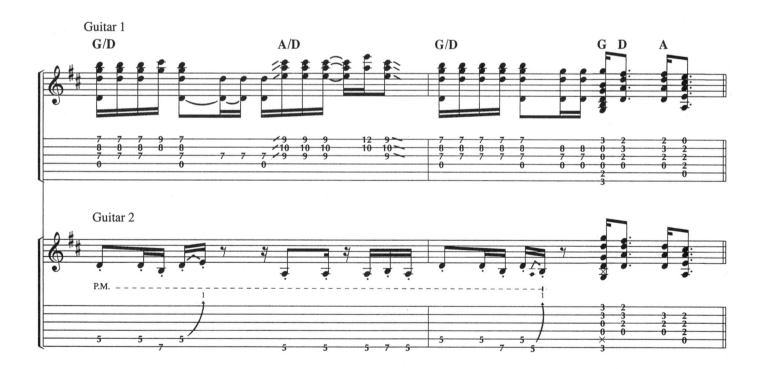

Verse 5:

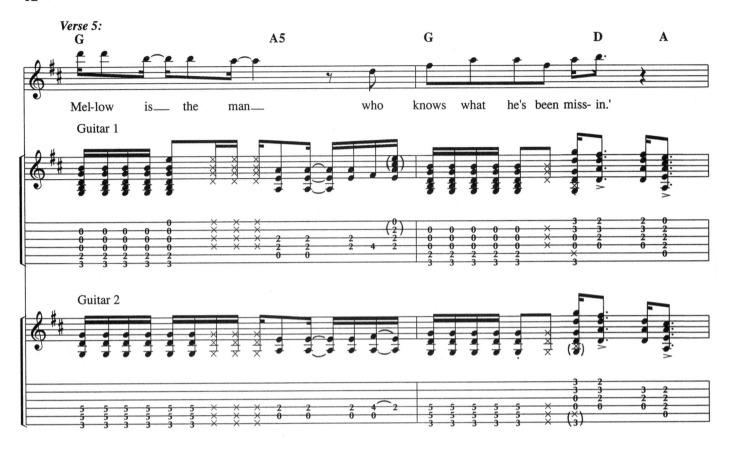

Mel-low is__ the man__ who knows what he's been miss- in.'

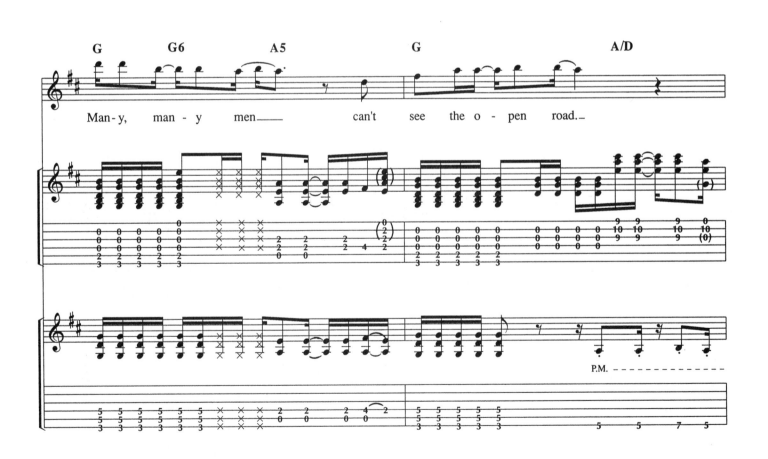

Man - y, man - y men__ can't see the o - pen road.__

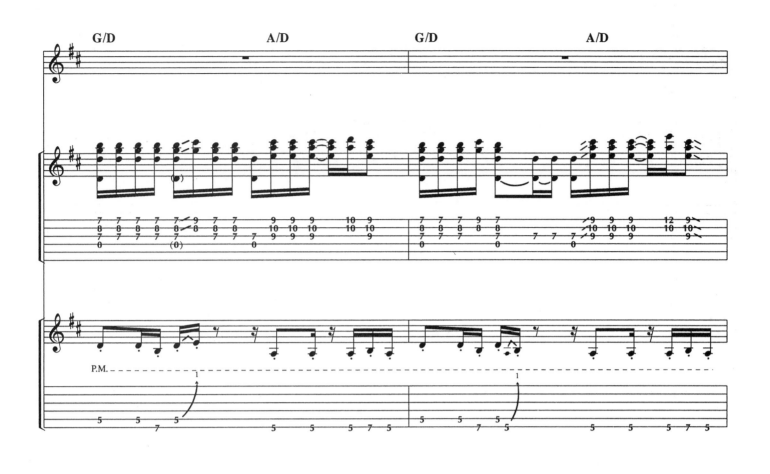

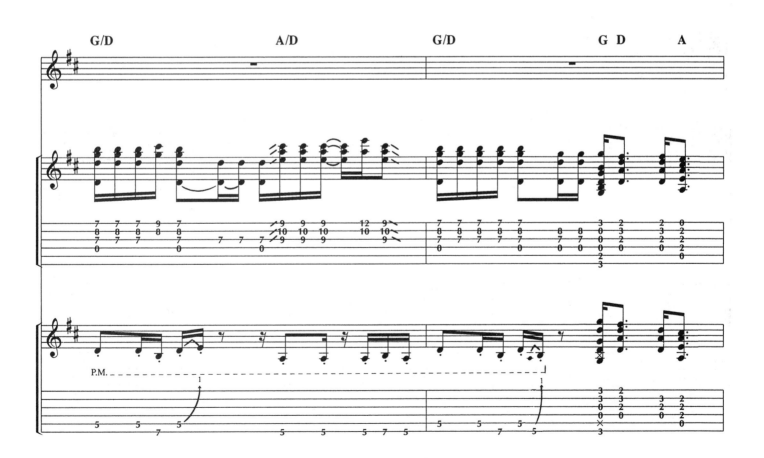

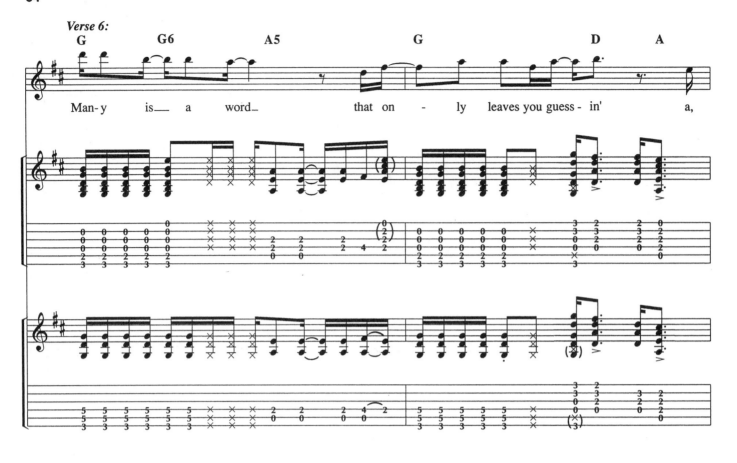

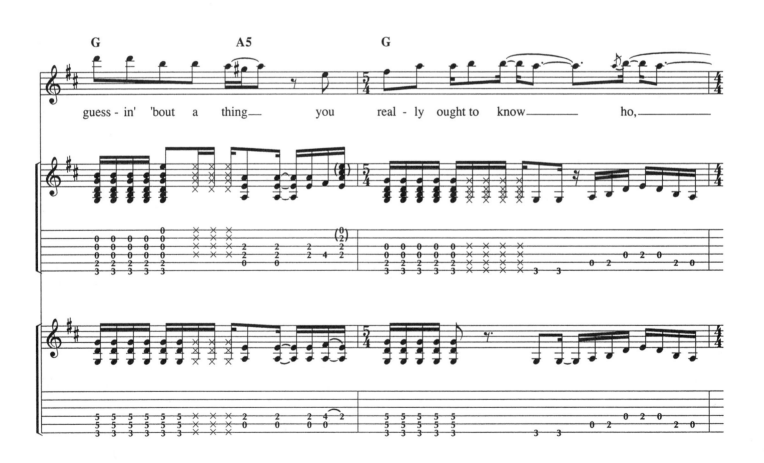

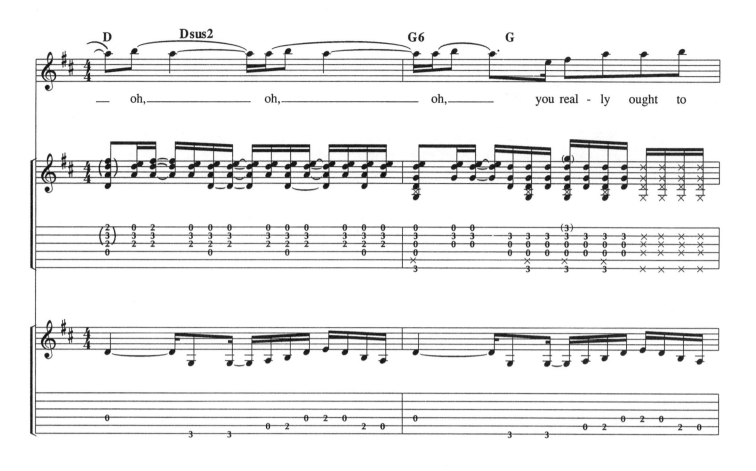

oh, _____ oh, _____ oh, _____ you real - ly ought to

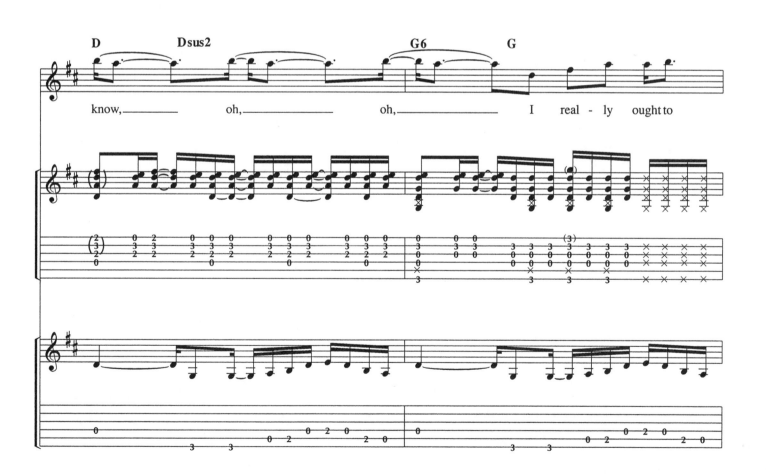

know, _____ oh, _____ oh, _____ I real - ly ought to

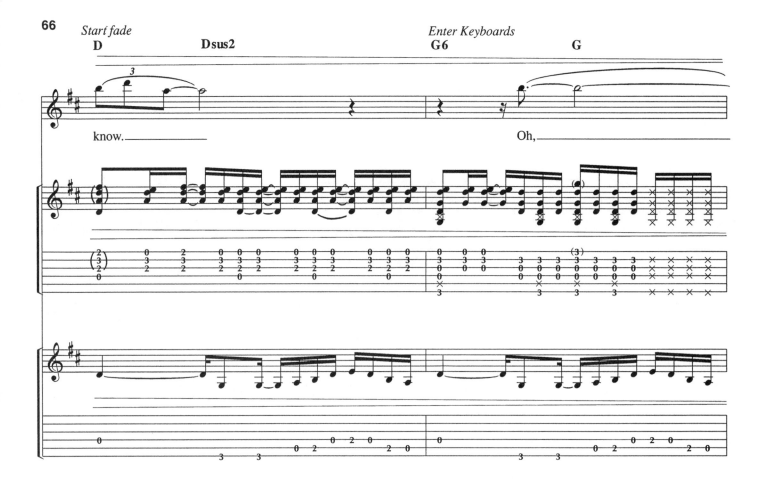

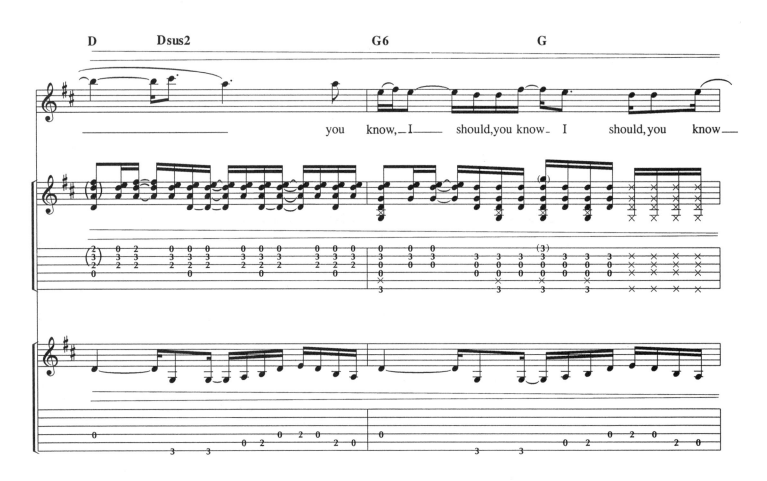

*Pedal Steel sounds arranged for Guitar.

THE CRUNGE

Words and Music by
**JOHN BONHAM, JOHN PAUL JONES,
JIMMY PAGE and ROBERT PLANT**

69

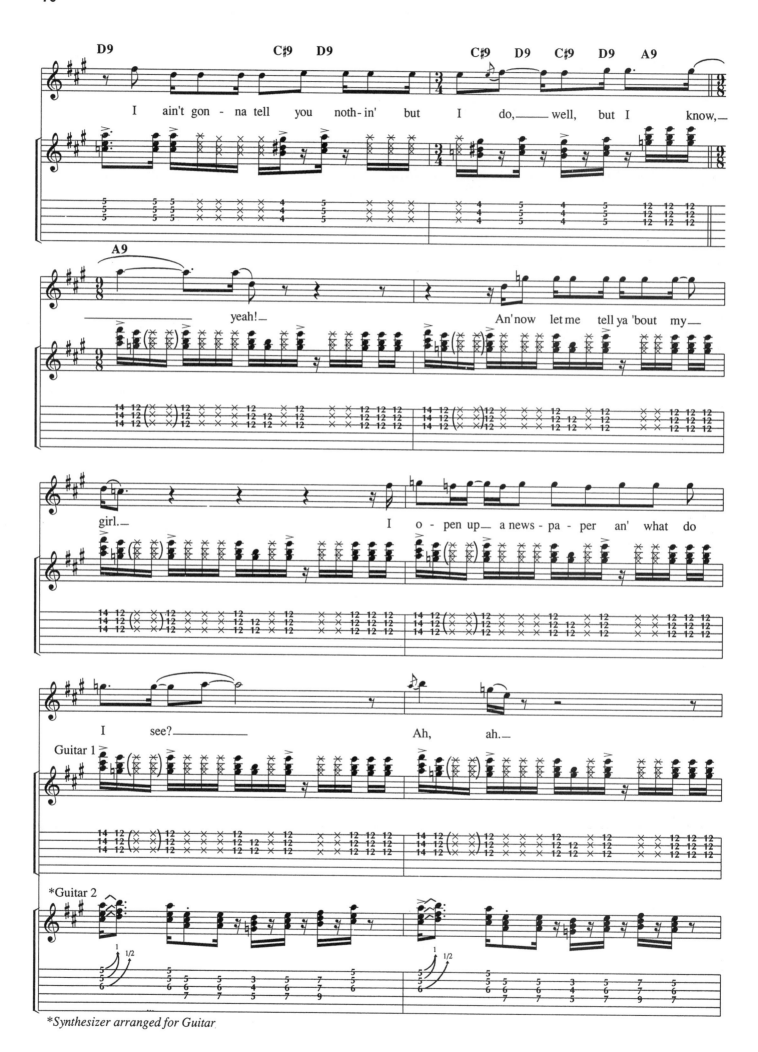

*Synthesizer arranged for Guitar.

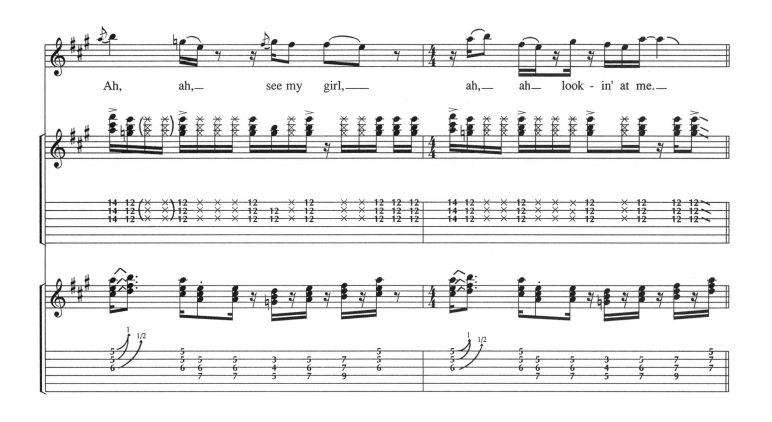

Ah, ah,— see my girl,— ah,— ah look - in' at me.—

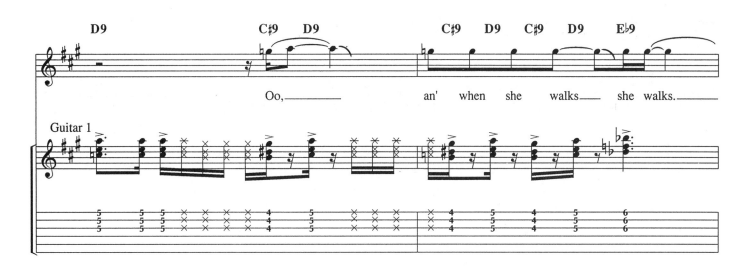

Oo,——— an' when she walks— she walks.———

Guitar 1

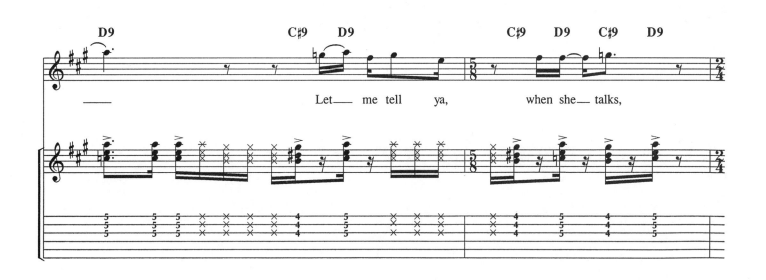

Let— me tell ya, when she— talks,

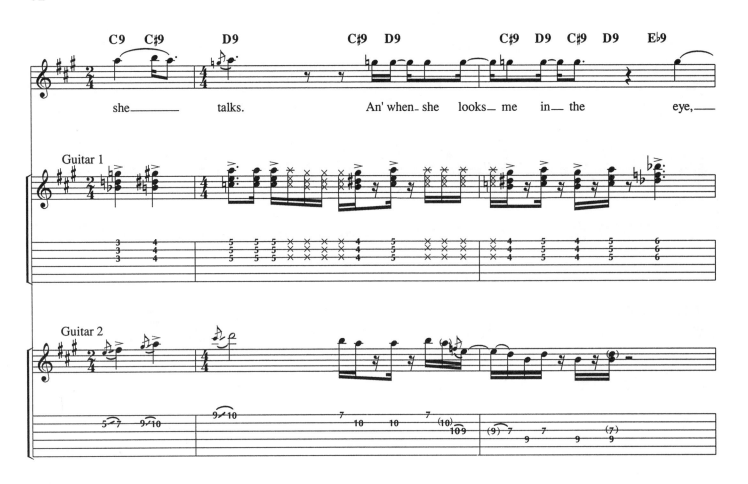

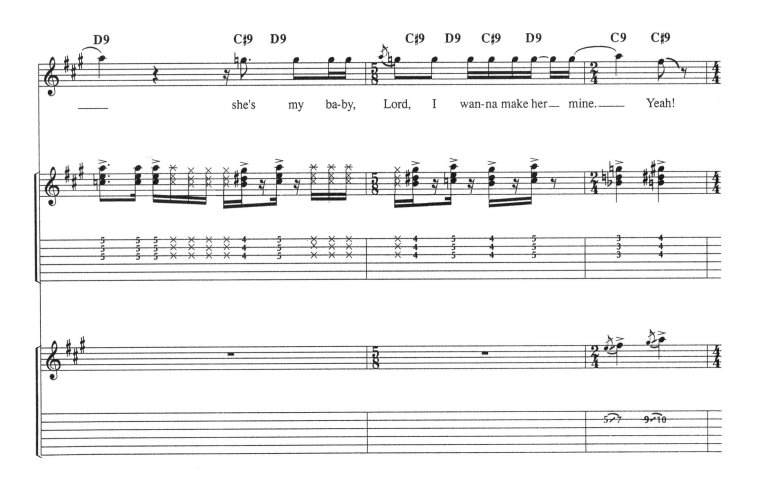

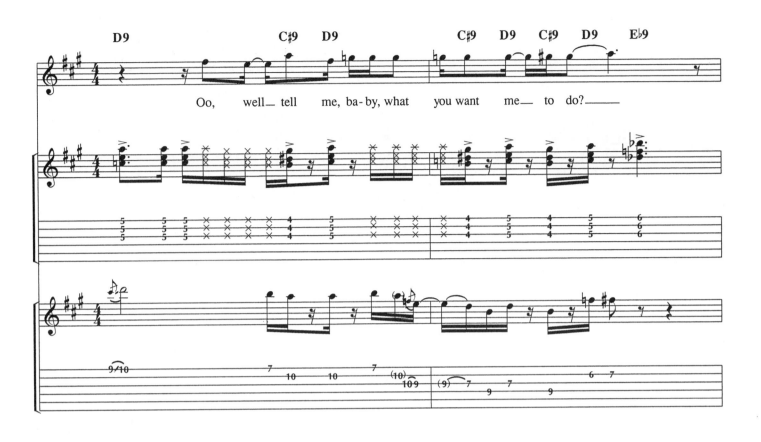

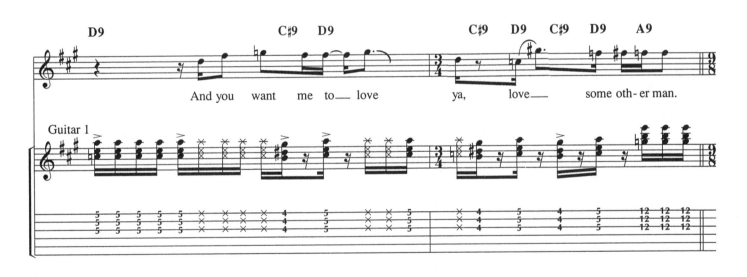

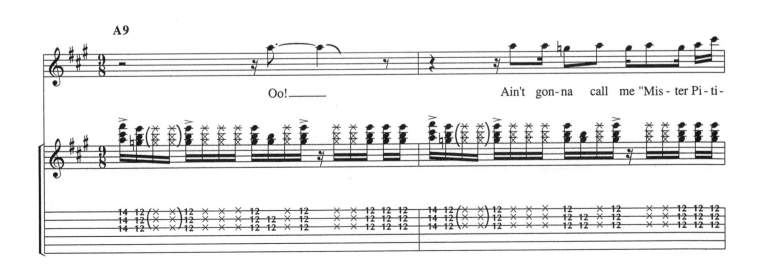

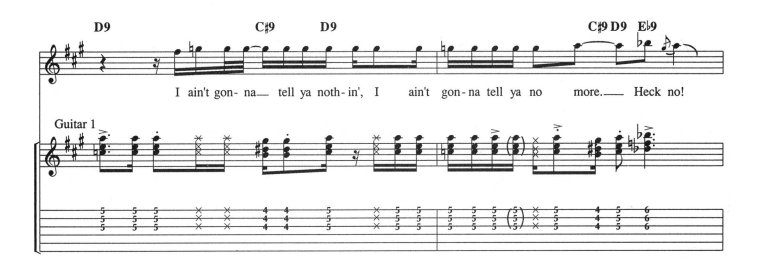

I ain't gon- na— tell ya noth- in', I ain't gon- na tell ya no more.— Heck no!

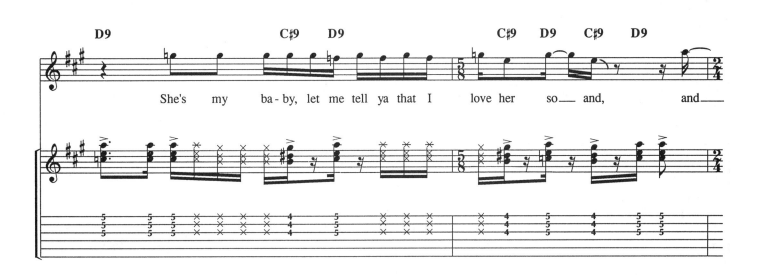

She's my ba- by, let me tell ya that I love her so— and, and—

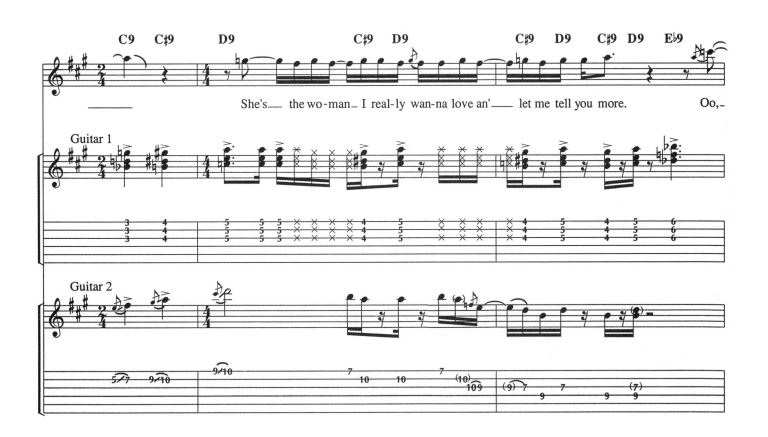

— She's— the wo- man— I real- ly wan- na love an'— let me tell you more. Oo,—

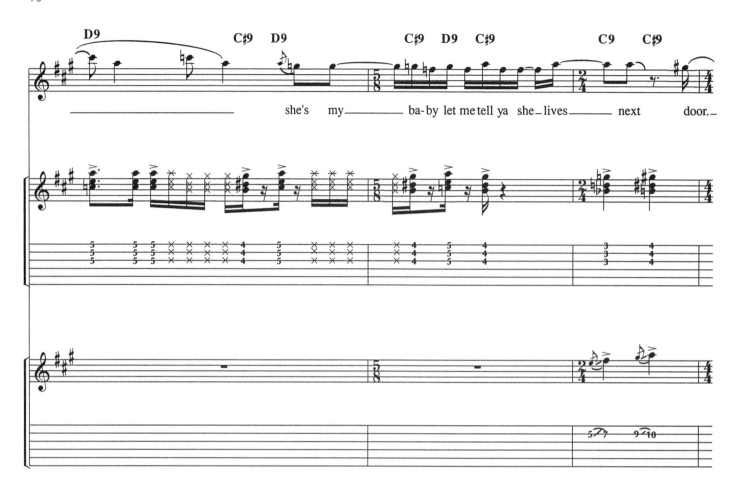

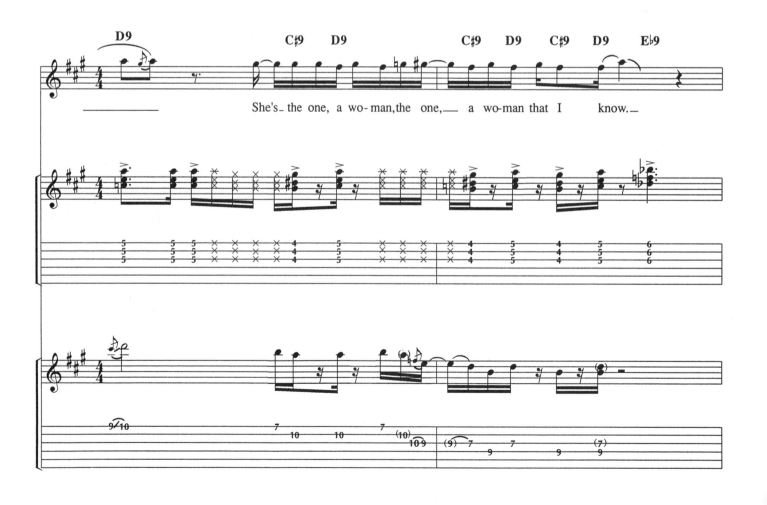

she's the kind of lov - er that__ makes__ me feel__ the whole__ world.

And__
(Steady gliss)

With bar

With bar

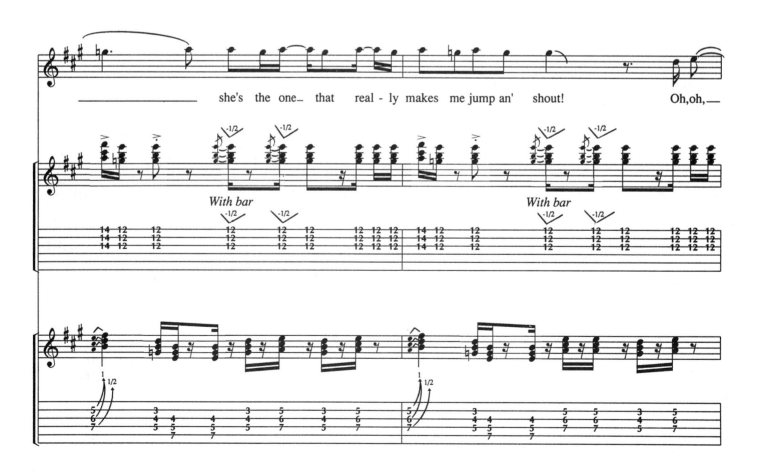

she's the one__ that real - ly makes me jump an' shout!

Oh, oh,__

With bar

With bar

she's the—kind of girl that I know what it's all a-bout.

Take it home,— take it, take it, take it.

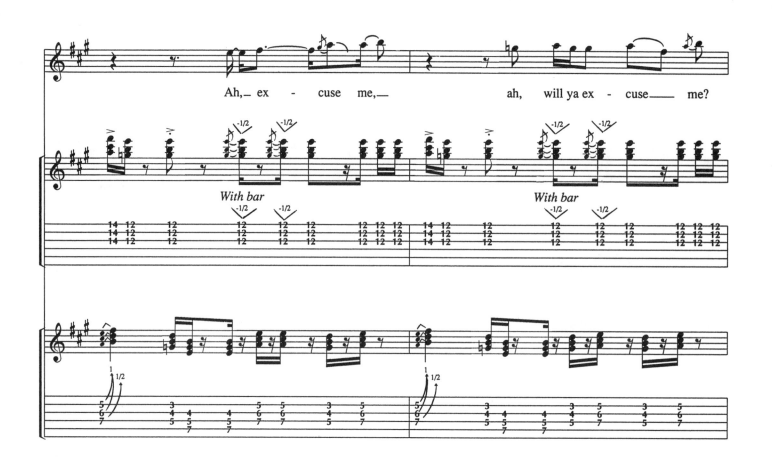

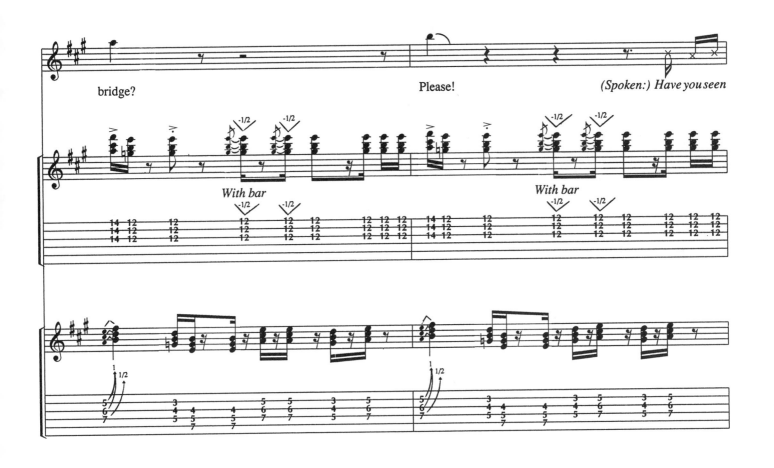

bridge?   Please!   *(Spoken:) Have you seen*

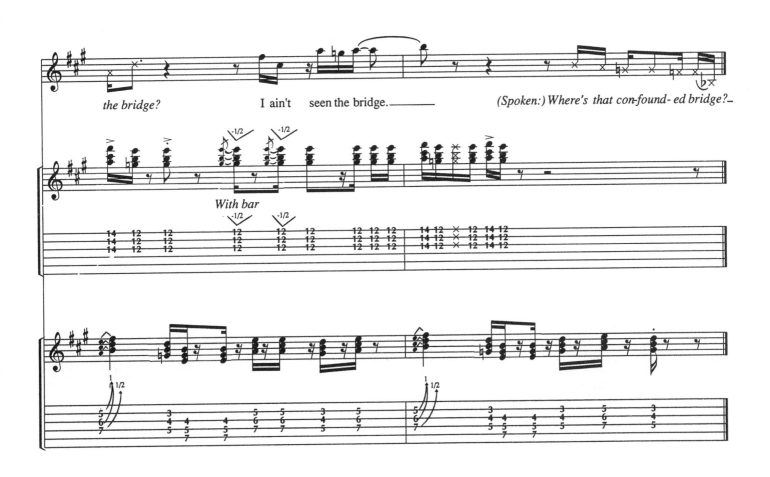

the bridge?   I ain't seen the bridge._____ *(Spoken:) Where's that con-found-ed bridge?_*

Dancing Days

Words and Music by
JIMMY PAGE and ROBERT PLANT

*In G tuning: ⑥ = D, ⑤ = G, ④ = D, ③ = G, ② = B, ① = D
**Overdub

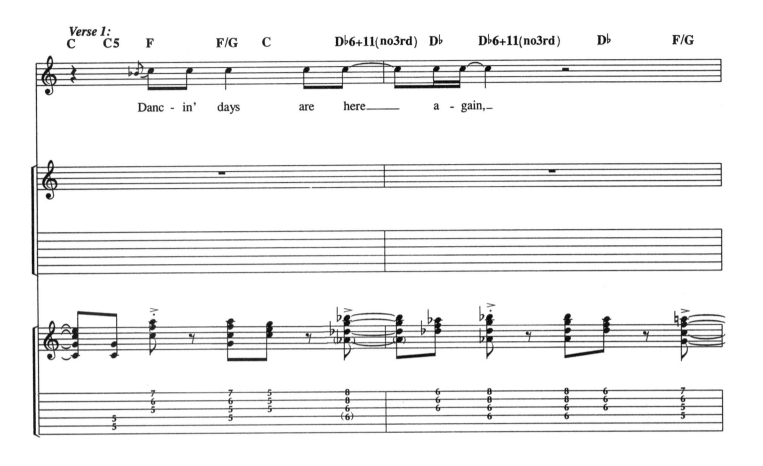

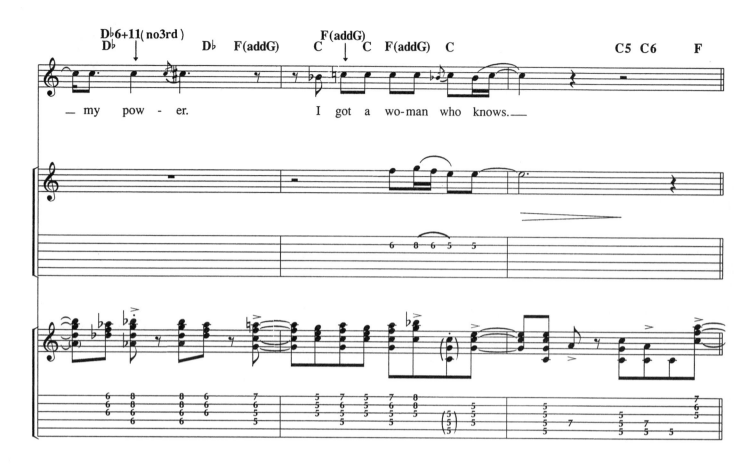

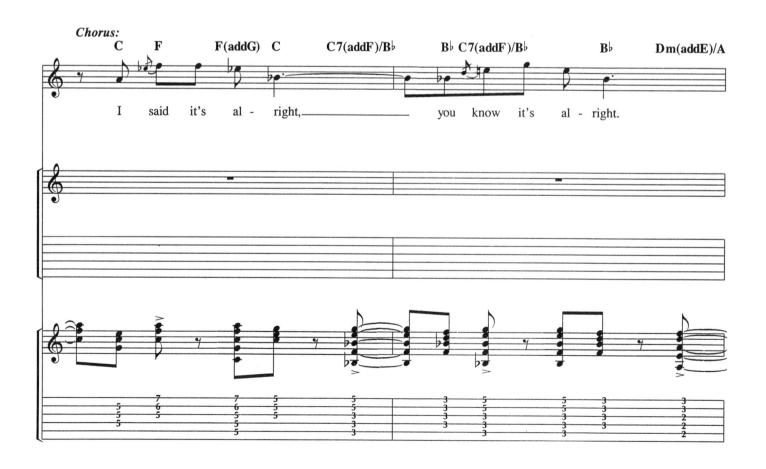

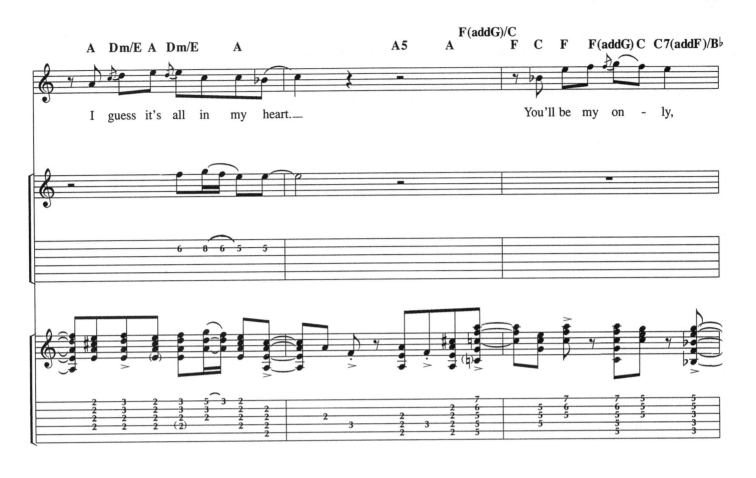

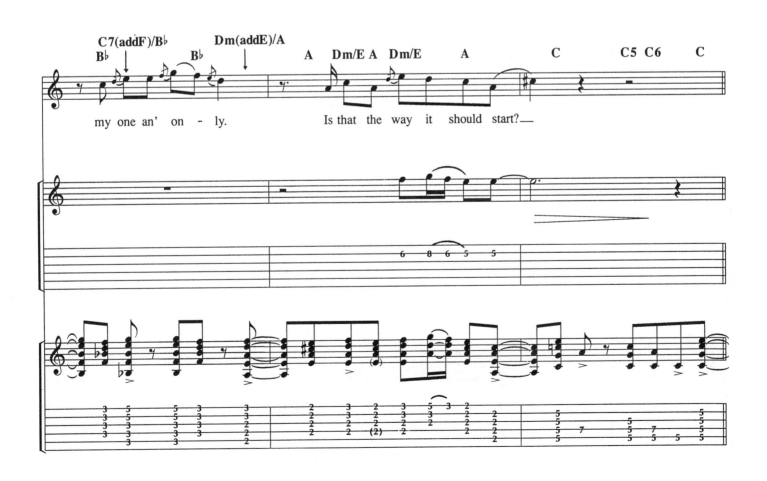

*Overdub

Verse 3:
*(Keyboards enter)

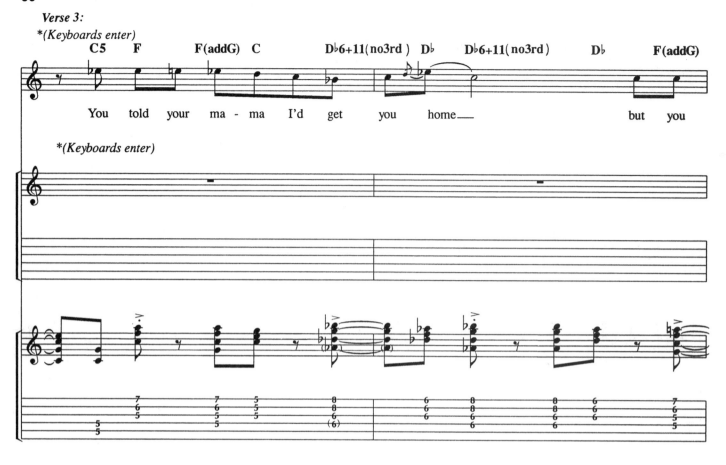

You told your ma-ma I'd get you home___ but you

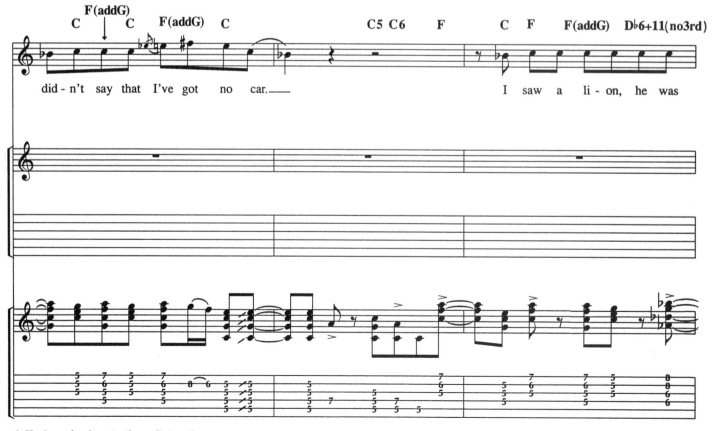

did-n't say that I've got no car.___ I saw a li-on, he was

* *Keyboards play simile to Guitar 2.*

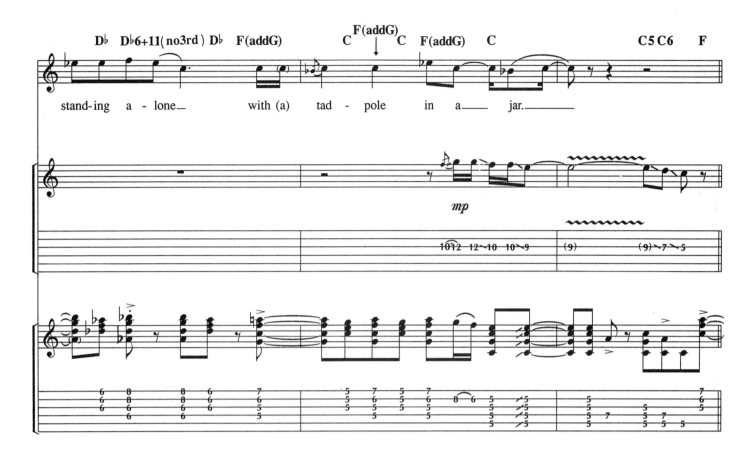

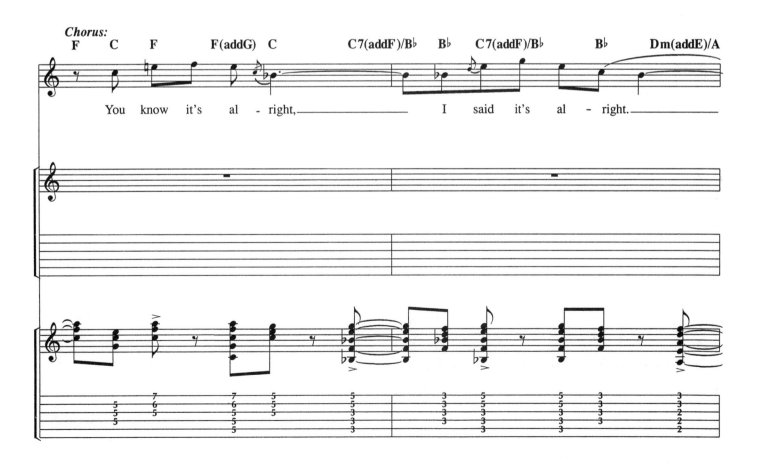

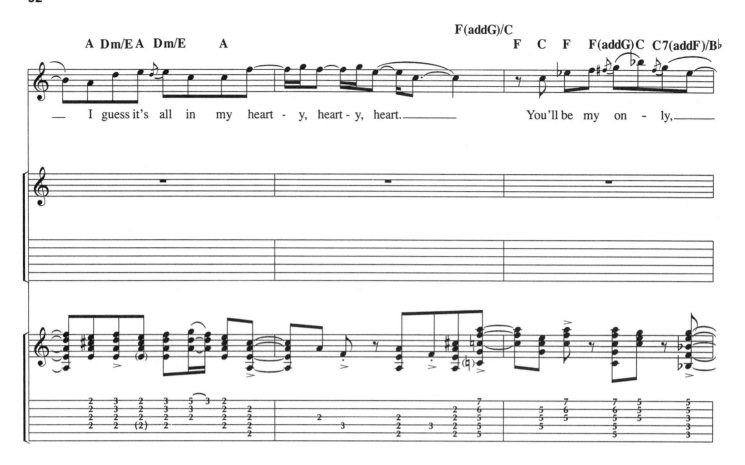

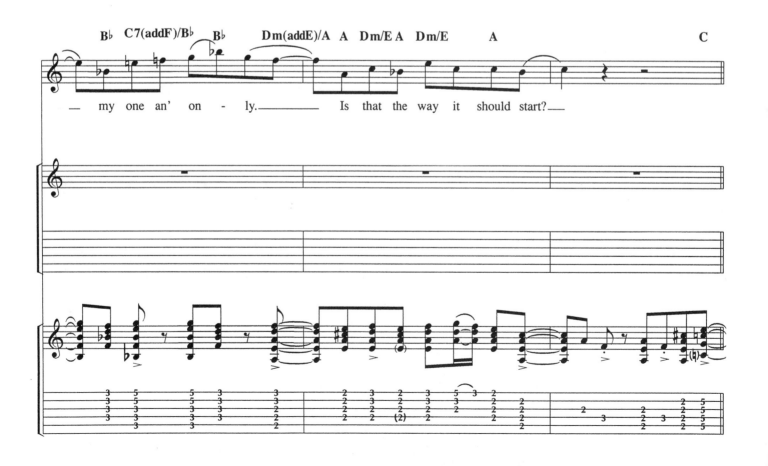

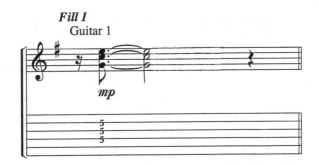

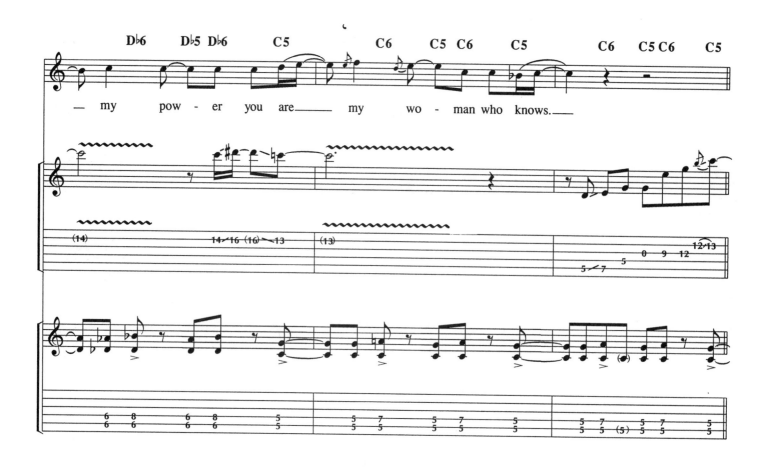

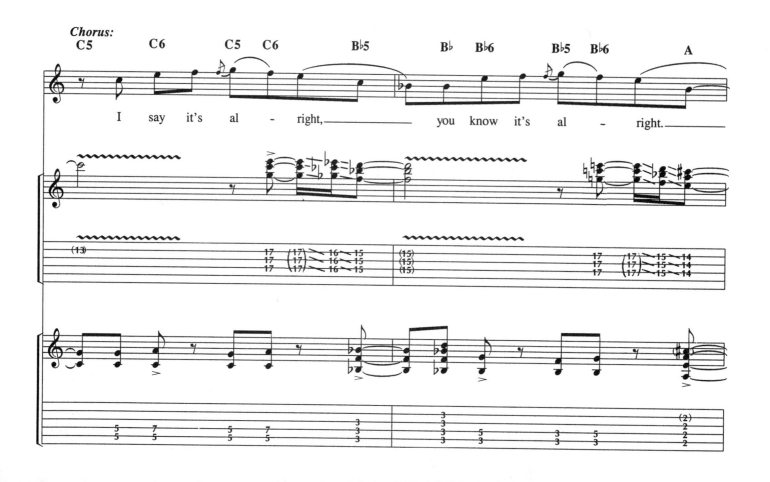

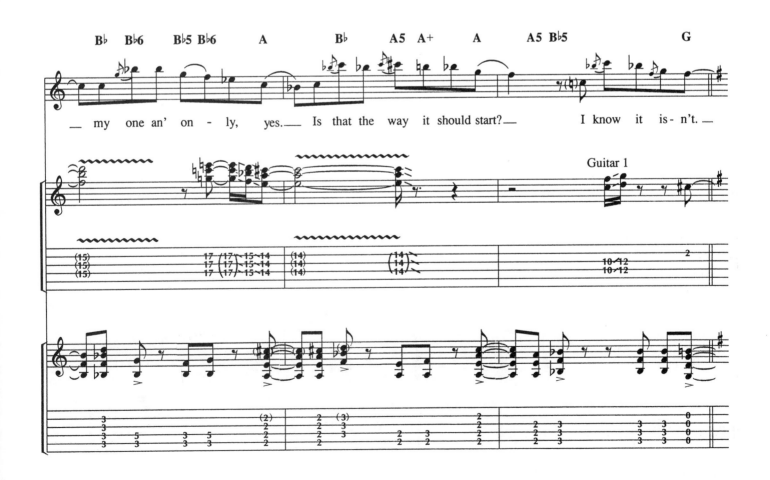

Interlude:

Guitar 1

Guitar 2

* Overdub

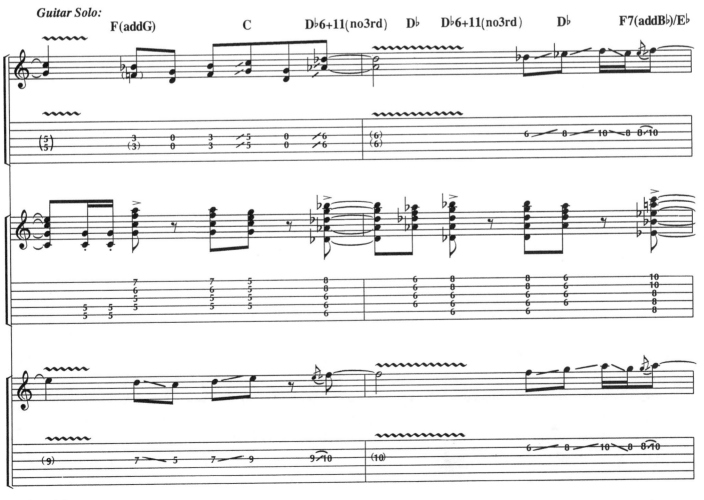

Overdub

Overdub

D'yer Maker

Words and Music by
JOHN BONHAM, JOHN PAUL JONES
and ROBERT PLANT

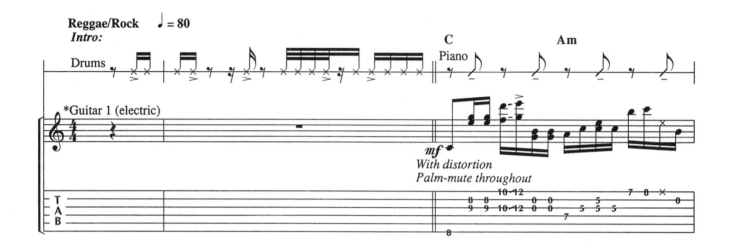

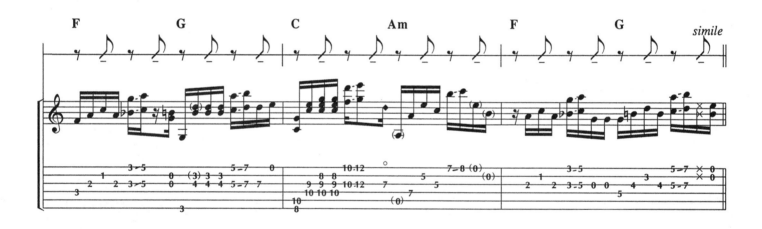

Tune down 1/4 tone to play with recording.

No Quarter

Words and Music by
JOHN PAUL JONES, JIMMY PAGE
and ROBERT PLANT

* *Electric Piano arranged for Guitar.*

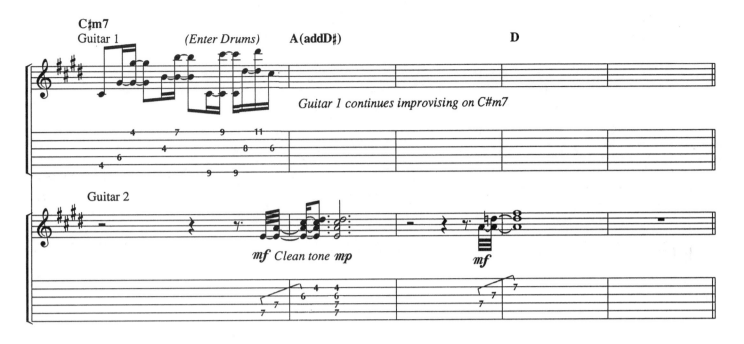

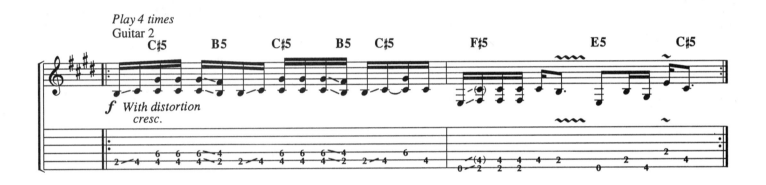

*Electric Piano (Guitar 1) only.

*Guitar 1 (Electric Piano) plays simile on repeats, improvising on C#m7
**1st time only
***Harmonic support by Keyboards. (C# Dorian / C# Aeolian)

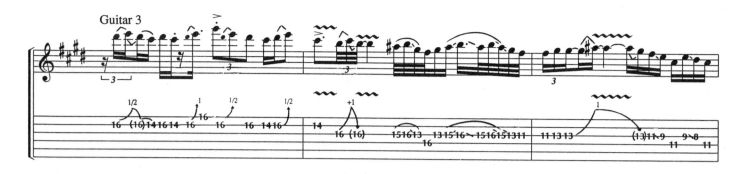

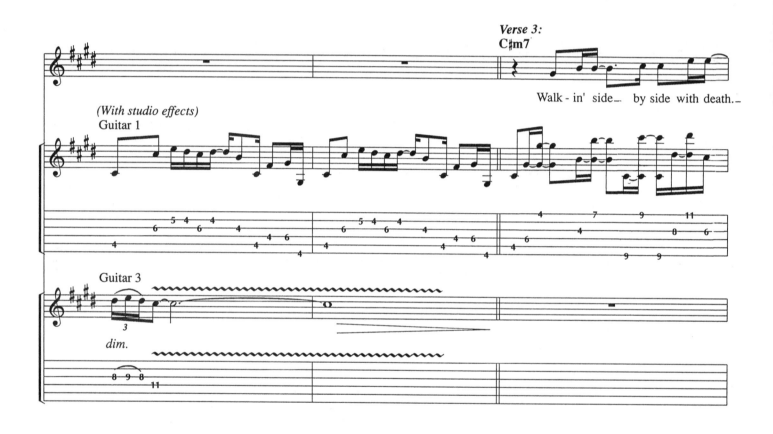

Verse 3:

Walk - in' side_ by side with death._

The dev-il mocks_their ev-'ry step._____ Oo._

*Doubled vocal starts and continues throughout with occassional low mixing.

The Ocean

Words and Music by
**JOHN BONHAM, JOHN PAUL JONES,
JIMMY PAGE and ROBERT PLANT**

*Slide to be played 1st time only.

122

124

*Chord suffixes in parethesis indicate composite harmony.

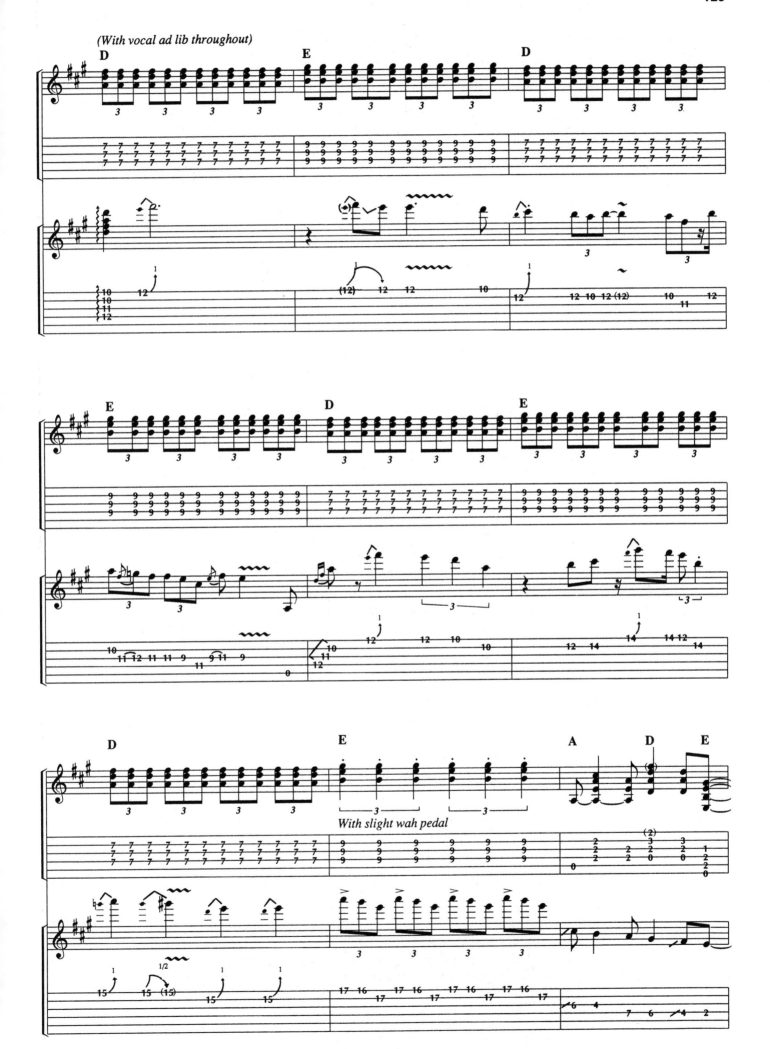

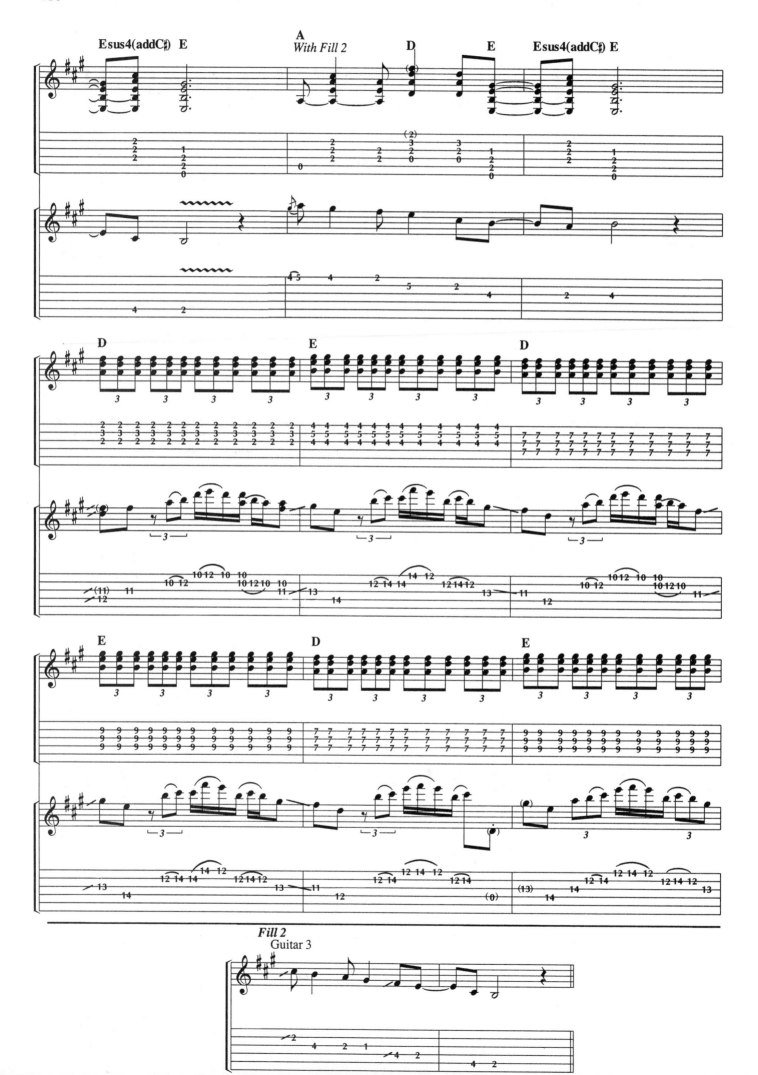

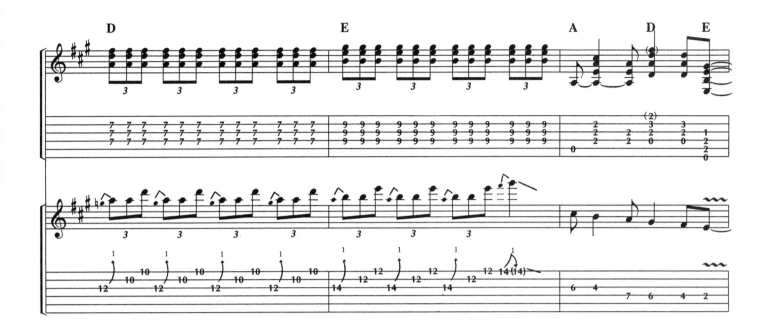

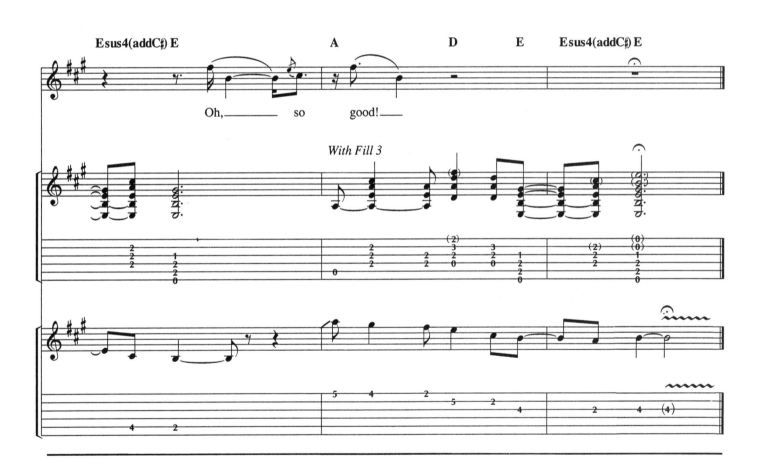

Oh,_____ so good!_____

Fill 3:
Guitar 3